CONTRAFLOW

LINES OF ENGLISHNESS
1922–2022

Contraflow

Lines of Englishness

1922–2022

SELECTED BY
JOHN GREENING AND
KEVIN GARDNER

FOREWORD BY
IAN McMILLAN

RENARD PRESS

RENARD PRESS LTD

124 City Road
London EC1V 2NX
United Kingdom
info@renardpress.com
020 8050 2928

www.renardpress.com

Contraflow first published by Renard Press Ltd in 2023

All poems © (for copyright holders and licensors please see 'Credits and
Permissions' on p. 330, which forms an extension of this copyright notice)
Selection, Notes and Introduction © John Greening and Kevin Gardner, 2023
Foreword © Ian McMillan, 2023

Design by Will Dady

Printed in the United Kingdom by Severn

ISBN: 978-1-80447-037-4

9 8 7 6 5 4 3 2 1

CONTENTS

FOREWORD

It seems to me that if you want to get to the essence of anything you go to poetry; here you will find nuance and transcendence and complexity as well as language turned up to the max. That's expected, of course, because poetry holds a torch up to the way we talk and think and write. You'd want nothing less for your time and concentration. All those words. All that beautiful white space.

I think, though, that you also go to poetry for history lessons, and maps of new and old geographies, and insights into how people who are very different to you lived their everyday lives. This book does just that; it uses poetry to seek out the essence of Englishness (or rather, essences of Englishnesses), which is perhaps something that only poetry can measure, since statistics might rust, the news can lose its newsiness and memory can be partial. And anyway, as Ezra Pound said, poetry is news that stays news. And he could have also said that poetry is statistics that always add up and poetry is a memory that never forgets.

It's true that as readers we often slide into an anthology knowing what to expect; we think that the book will be organised in a certain, roughly predictable, way. It will be chronological. It will be alphabetical. It will be organised thematically. The brilliant organising principle behind this *Contraflow* is there in the title: the work is in two timelines running in different directions which meet in the middle. Poems from the 1920s rub stanzas with poems from the 2020s, poems from the 1950s with the 1990s and so on. The almost miraculous effect of this is that it makes the reader examine the poems of each decade in the direct sunlight of the other, and it enhances the complexity of the task at hand.

Concerns are seen to echo concerns, styles and ideas are seen to predate other styles and ideas, and increasing diversity has a satnav that plots its direction. Poem-pebbles land in the pool of *Contraflow* and the ripples spread in every direction, as the ripples of poems always do; in this case they criss-cross the timelines of Englishness as represented in poetry like timelords might.

This scaffolding means that *Contraflow* is packed with marvellous poetic examinations of Englishness – what is it, how does it work, how can we measure it? Here we'll find poems attempting to answer that question from many decades: a 1930s C. Day Lewis 'You that love England, who have an ear for her music,/The slow movement of clouds in benediction,/Clear arias of light thrilling over her uplands,/Over the chords of summer sustained peacefully'; and a 2020s Zaffar Kunial 'an impossible interior, deeper than forests/ and further in...' In this corner of England there's Carol Rumens in the 1980s 'When you're an adult, life's all O level/Stay clear of children, keep your figures nice!' and in this other corner of England there's Sylvia Townsend Warner in the 1920s observing (or perhaps imagining) 'The congregation coming out after morning prayer/ with loitering alacrity they trooped out into the air.' Each of these places exists in reality, and each of them constitute an England of the mind and in poetry they can both coexist.

So when you read this book and take your time with reading over subject areas and time-stanzas you'll realise, as I did, that there are as many Englishnesses as there are poems about Englishness. And the beauty of an anthology like this is that you can turn it like a kaleidoscope and the poems will land in different formations, or you can read it from beginning to end and a narrative will emerge. Or you can do both, and Englishnesses will melt into each other or will form a queue, each one bumping into the next.

I used to have a photograph of my dad, a proud Scotsman, standing on the England side of the England–Scotland border with his thumb pointing downwards and a grimace on his Lanarkshire face; he knew that he was enacting a species of cultural cartoon that only had about one dimension, but he did it anyway. He pretended, with a twinkle in his eye, that he saw Englishness as something other, as something outside, as something across the border. The other side of that crude coin would be someone stepping over the border and greeting the camera with a broad grin and a thumbs-up, and the beauty of this book is that it looks, poetically, at both sides of the coin.

For some people Englishness is a kind of religion, for others it's a state of mind that makes them a little uncomfortable, and this book examines both those worlds; there are poems like Hannah Lowe's brilliant 'The Only English Kid', about the eponymous child in the class who, in a discussion about race and racism 'would sit there quietly, looking guilty/for all the awful things he hadn't done', and poems like Carol Ann Duffy's 'White Cliffs': 'Something fair and strong implied in chalk,/what we might wish ourselves', and poems like John Betjeman's 'Middlesex', which begins 'Gaily into Ruislip Gardens/Runs the red electric train,/With a thousand Ta's and Pardon's/Daintily alights Elaine.' Englishness is somewhere in the middle of the worlds these poems are building, in the spaces between stanzas, in the images and the rhymes.

I've read this anthology quite a few times as I thought about this foreword. I read it as summer turned to autumn and the leaves fell off the trees like poems from an endless collection. I read it on crowded trains as they sped into tunnels that throbbed with metaphor. I read it in Cleethorpes at my mother-in-law's caravan on a wet and windy afternoon. I read it sitting on a bench in a London park. I read it as my newest grandson slept beside me on the settee. Each time I read it and each place I read it in added to the prism of Englishness through which I viewed the world. My dad would be laughing.

What are you waiting for? Jump in!

IAN MCMILLAN
Darfield, Barnsley, 2022

A CONVERSATION ABOUT
ENGLISHNESS

'Stilled legendary depth:
It was as deep as England.'
– Ted Hughes

JG: When I tell people we've been editing a collection of poems about Englishness, there's often an awkward silence. It's understandable. At best, they may be imagining something tub-thumping and nostalgic – the kind of patriotic anthology Edward Thomas was obliged to edit before he enlisted. At worst, they might feel we're stirring up a toxic brew of nationalism. What they won't necessarily realise is how complex and many-faceted the idea of Englishness has become since Thomas was writing.

KG: To be fair, I had no idea myself before we started this project. I think I must have expected poetry about Englishness to play endless variations on Thomas's elegiac vision – 'The horses started and for the last time/I watched the clods crumble and topple over/After the ploughshare and the stumbling team' – or on Betjeman's nostalgia for a 'lost Elysium'. The tumults of more recent years have surely had an indelible effect.

JG: Quite apart from Brexit and the recent change of monarch, there have been so many cultural upheavals in my lifetime. And in the period we're looking at – a hundred years – well, for example, think how the industrial landscape has been transformed. True, Lieutenant Thomas might possibly recognise that other more traditional rural landscape, but he'd find the robotic technology in today's depopulated, hedgeless English fields more reminiscent of the battlefield. Then, all the behavioural shifts – our suspicion of deference, the increasing candour about sex, a general slackening of that stiff upper lip. Although it certainly hasn't vanished, there has been a steady erosion of the class system. Homosexuality is no longer entirely in the closet. Women have been empowered (especially women poets). Empire has all but gone, and multiculturalism has arrived. Many people won't realise that some of the most striking poetry about English identity from the past fifty years has been from Black and Asian writers. But the poetry they write is changing – the tranquil pastoral note Zaffar Kunial strikes in his wonderful 2022 collection, *England's Green*, for example, is something Edward Thomas would surely have appreciated. In one of the poems, Kunial finds 'the whole of unknown/England' pulled out of the air by the memory of a hedgerow. But I suspect that a Texan has a slightly different angle on all this?

KG: I suppose one might well ask whether an American is in a position to know anything at all about Englishness, anything beyond superficial emblems – White Cliffs, red telephone boxes, Trooping the Colour, stiff upper lips, Manchester United, clotted cream. Of course, those things aren't Englishness itself, merely instances of what Englishness might mean to an outsider. But such clichés quickly show the difficulty in what we set out to do: the problem of defining an abstraction of nationhood by way of concrete examples. Any list of English national traits, experiences or qualities is necessarily limited.

JG: You've hit the nail on the head – which is why it's great to have a transatlantic perspective.

KG: I recall an early proposal for this anthology in which we selected for chapter headings such characteristics as

Eccentrics, Embarrassment, Fair Play, the English Abroad, As Others See Us, Food and Drink, Class, Honours, Disgrace and so on. Yet no matter how many categories we chose, and no matter how many poems we identified that seemed to speak to these topics, this approach never actually defined Englishness; it was never more than the sum of its parts – perhaps slightly less! It seemed (to this American, at least) that there is an Englishness, but that it has little to do with national eccentricities. My own sense – and do tell me if you disagree – is that Englishness, at least in the poems we've gathered here, can be summed up in the sense of 'not what we used to be', whatever that was, and is generally expressed with a melancholy long withdrawing roar.

JG: I suspect Larkin might have expressed it more pithily than Arnold. There's the roar, yes, but the yelp and the snarl too. Though not so much Whitman's 'barbaric yawp'.

KG: Larkin could certainly snarl, but just as frequent is a plaintive lament: 'And that will be England gone,/The shadows, the meadows, the lanes/The guildhalls, the carved choirs.' In any case, I'll confess I've never had much taste for the yawps and howls of American poetry. My preference is for elegy and pastoral, which English poets do so well.

JG: And which your beloved Betjeman brought to perfection – but he could 'put the boot in' too. There's a very English tradition of satire, which is alive and well, and we do represent that here. You're right about our instinct for nostalgia, though – the English are good at elegy, undoubtedly, and the tug of it is even there in that song from oh-so-English *Salad Days*: 'We said we'd never look back...'

KG: Well, here I reveal my ignorance of Englishness. I take it that *Salad Days* is a musical of some sort, but not one I have ever heard of.

JG: It was premiered in the year of my birth, so it's fairly ancient. We used to listen to scratchy old records of the songs or sing along with my mother at the piano. *Salad Days* was popular here – it captured that breezy never-had-it-so-good post war optimism of the 50s – but it was fairly unexportable. More insular Englishness. You know, it makes sense to be editing this together, because I feel that Americans don't rely so much on the rear-view mirror and rather 'tell it like it is' – something the foggy English are *not* good at. We prefer to gaze indecisively at our clotted cream. 'Indecisiveness' might even have been a chapter theme. Wasn't one of the poems we considered P.J. Kavanagh's 'Edward Thomas in Heaven', where he tries to imagine Thomas in a world without uncertainty?

KG: And as you once reminded me, it was Thomas who inspired a certain American friend to immortalise that 'road not taken'. But what really intrigues me is why Edward Thomas is such an inescapable figure for so many English writers over the past hundred years. Is there something in his simple touchstones – an empty platform, willow-herb, haycocks, high clouds and a blackbird that defines the English soul? Of all the poems that are built on a sudden memory of an unremarkable place, why does 'Adlestrop' have such extraordinary pull?

JG: I think it may be to do with the Beeching cuts to the railways. I remember sending you a link at one point to Flanders and Swann's wonderful and moving song, 'The Slow Train', whose lyrics we might almost have included. But there's certainly a love of trains in England – something else Betjeman understood, and it helped him capture the hearts of many thousands of commuters: 'Gaily into Ruislip Gardens/Runs the red electric train…' We lived near Ruislip, and my father used to love those poems.

KG: 'With a thousand Ta's and Pardon's, daintily alights Elaine.' It's magical stuff, and it explains why few other poets have been as influential as Betjeman in defining Englishness for the English.

JG: At least, the southern English; there's less to appeal in him beyond the Home Counties, perhaps – although I hope we have represented the whole of England here. I'm conscious of some inevitable gaps, but this was never meant to be a geographical survey. No call for a gazetteer, as we had in our country-house anthology, *Hollow Palaces*.

KG: What about when it comes to defining Englishness for other poets? My sense is that Edward Thomas may have earned those laurels. Perhaps his death at Arras in World War I enshrined his notions of Englishness for future poets?

JG: Brooke's death had the more immediate and widespread effect. Sadly he wasn't such a good poet, just a well-connected one. Thomas has undoubtedly been a huge stylistic influence – that conversational note, which was largely absent from English poetry before he and Frost perfected it.

KG: I do hope we've managed to avoid replicating Brooke's 'forever England' and 'English heaven' nonsense. Though there are times it feels we may have gone journeying with H. V. Morton *In Search of England*. Not a bad journey to make, if one could.

JG: My wife has a teetering pile of Morton – a difficult man, but full of insight in his writings. I'm not sure he'd have liked *Contraflow*...

KG: Well, our book is not heading in entirely the same direction as Morton's. But I do believe there's an almost instinctive yearning for, or belief in, an elusive England, rendered hazily pastoral in the imagination. Do you remember when Michael Wood revived Morton's title for a book and television series popular about twenty years ago? Wood spoke to the English sense that the real England could only be found by journeying into the past. Perhaps the quest for a 'past perfect' is really a journey into an England of the mind. Glyn Hughes hits on this instinct: 'All revives the yearning/that lures us back to a seeming peace.' Yet so much of *Contraflow* looks in the opposite direction from Morton and Wood.

JG: One of our aims here was to show how English poetry has developed through the last century. Do you think, though, there's more to be learned from the Second than the First World War? A recent essay of mine[1] looks briefly at *England: An Anthology*, which was published in 1944 by 'a committee of the English Association' (of which I was once a Fellow, as it happens). It's largely the work of dead white males, but Harold Nicolson's introduction does have some relevant things to say about Englishness. What we've found in our foraging is much more diverse, but there is, I think you'll agree, what he called a 'resonant continuity of tone', even when the style is as arrestingly contemporary as in, say, Glyn Maxwell or Jo Shapcott.

KG: That's a useful phrase – 'resonant continuity of tone'. It may be the one common thread among our endlessly varied selections. But that phrase also exposes a difficulty within our selections: are we aiming to show continuity or divergence – or both?

JG: I keep thinking of Danny Boyle's opening ceremony to the 2012 London Olympics – absolutely modern, yet Shakespeare and Chaucer would have loved it. You're right, of course, about those slightly desperate categories we considered, which are not so different from the 1944 ones, in fact. We were in danger of producing *England's Most Beautiful Poems* or *England: A Book to Remember Her By*. Maybe it was looking at that anthology which persuaded me to risk the intricate layout we finally opted for in *Contraflow*. The opposing chronologies are a helpfully thorough way of ploughing our particular field. But the topics for each decade do, I hope, avoid the obvious. They were chosen quickly, instinctively, rather than through long meditation or discussion – though we had many long talks about what approach to take. And at

---

1 'A Condition of England', *Poetry Birmingham Literary Journal*, Vol. 8 (Summer 2022).

times it has seemed as though we were loading ourselves with chains and trying to get out of them.

KG: It did seem so at times. In response to your earlier question, I think you've hit on a key issue when you suggest we might learn more from the Second World War than the First. It's a perplexing fact that English poetry seems unable to escape the ghosts of the Great War. But I think that what World War II did to the face of the nation and to its culture and economy has had a much more significant impact on how poets portray England and Englishness. World War I resulted in the loss of a generation, but it could be said that England still looked and felt like England in its aftermath. World War II, in contrast, shattered many traditional English signifiers and, almost simultaneously, began to introduce many new cultural markers.

JG: Not least the arrival of a new queen, who had an extraordinarily long reign ahead of her. Charles Tomlinson – who from the 1950s was writing marvellously about Englishness but always liked to swim against the current – has a little piece from 2006 that is a reminder of how much changed:

I Was a Child

> when I played Tasmania
> in the Empire Day pageant:
> that was May twenty-fourth – Victoria's
> birthday, another age in fact
> and the old queen's head
> still reigned on half the currency:
> as I climbed up to the stage
> robed and shoeless,
> a splinter from the floor
> penetrated my naked foot as keen
> as a Tasmanian arrow.[2]

---

2 Charles Tomlinson, 'I Was a Child', *Cracks in the Universe* (Manchester: Carcanet, 2006).

I think that splinter marked the end of Empire. At the same time, the Commonwealth was strengthened, and (most importantly) the colonial balance was redressed, so that people who had lived under British sway were entitled to settle here. Suddenly a multicultural society began to take root, and the poetry of the time starts to reflect it.

KG: It does seem sudden, doesn't it? Though there were signs of this sea change coming. It may have taken some time to realise the vision, but as far back as 1713 Pope seems to have predicted the Windrush generation:

> Whole nations enter with each swelling tyde,
> And seas but join the regions they divide;
> Earth's distant ends our glory shall behold,
> And the new world launch forth to seek the old.

That prophecy touches on a major kind of Englishness in the poetry of the 50s and 60s. And our sense of a shift in representations of Englishness certainly contributed to the idea of structuring the anthology with counter-flowing directions.

JG: Yes, I'm not quite sure how that idea first swam into our ken, but rather than deserted railway stations I think motorways may have had something to do with it. You won't know about this, Kevin, but John Major's notorious 'Cones Hotline' was designed to alert drivers to road repairs and contraflow systems when he was Prime Minister in 1992, but the public simply mocked the scheme out of existence – Pope would certainly have written a few couplets on it. Nevertheless, it's precisely that image of intertwining traffic that gives our book its structure: two chronologies working with and against each other, a century of poets heading from and to all points of the compass. Curiously enough, some of those aerial shots of the queue for the Queen's lying-in-state conveyed very much the same image. As a structural device it seemed a way of escaping the weary categories and at the same time exploring unexpected corners of English poetry. You may remember, it was also Major who evoked this 'country of long shadows on county grounds, warm beer, invincible green suburbs, dog lovers and pools fillers'. He called it Britain, but the scene felt very English. And not necessarily welcoming to outsiders who may not even know that 'pools' are for betting on football matches (one German translator of Larkin's 'Mr Bleaney' translated 'He kept on plugging at the four aways' as 'He took four holidays a year'). But secret codes and passwords are another aspect of Englishness: knowing how to pronounce Magdalene or Cholmondeley or indeed Featherstonehaugh ('Fanshaw', I'm told).

KG: There are landmines aplenty, especially for the unsuspecting American. Some may just be quirks of regional pronunciation, like Happisburgh or Shrewsbury. (We have those, too. Good luck with Natchitoches!) But it's the wilfully, perversely twisted battle between spelling and upper-class pronunciation that I think you're getting at. Like Leveson-Gower, or half the names in Wodehouse.

JG: It's an offshoot of the class system. I'm rather sorry we didn't have room in the end for Wendy Cope's brilliant Larkin parody, 'Mr Strugnell', but I suppose we were wary of too many poems about poets. But perhaps we should talk about the whole business of getting a balance of men and women and the challenges that presents when looking at a hundred years of poetry…?

KG: I think we've been quite judicious in that regard, and not just out of a dutiful commitment to representation. That the earlier decades – especially the 40s – are as strong in female voices as the more recent ones indicates that an interest in Englishness is not the sole preserve of white, male, Oxbridge poets.

JG: That has been quite a revelation, though some of the women poets are still hard to track down. The canon of World War I poetry was dramatically reshaped by a single anthology, *Scars Upon My Heart*,[3] but later decades are still awaiting that kind of reappraisal. There have been rediscoveries such as Rosemary Tonks, but others like Margaret Stanley-Wrench remain in the shadows, along with Molly Holden, Frances Bellerby, Robert Bridges's daughter Elizabeth Daryush and Lilian Bowes Lyon – even though she's a relative of the King's.

KG: Equally exciting to discover that many poets of colour have also contemplated the subject. As you said from the outset, we've brought together a quite varied array of representations of Englishness and attitudes toward it, yet few reliable patterns emerged that indicated gendered or racial ways of looking at the subject. As you rightly noted, John, it certainly wasn't all melancholy for lost intangibles, but even when that was the theme, it was sometimes surprising to find who was expressing that nostalgia. Kamau Brathwaite, in 'Conqueror' (a poem we had hoped to include), approaches Englishness 'From quiet shires of church bells', while Derek Walcott hears 'the drone of the abbeys from matins to compline'. But then there are also the lively celebrations of a new England – one where colour has replaced the grey-tone drabness of post-war England, an England dressed in 'salwar kameez/peacock-blue//embossed slippers, gold and black//an apple-green sari,/silver-bordered' (Alvi), an England addressed by 'battered envelopes/postmarked Srinigar, Ramallah, Grozny' (Dharker), an England of 'Grey light and close skies', but also of 'chokey streets, roundabouts and streetlamps/with tyres chucked round them' (D'Aguiar). This is a new English pastoral; a shift has occurred, but it's almost too gradual to pinpoint.

---

3 Catherine Reilly, *Scars Upon My Heart* (Virago, 1981).

JG: I agree that there is a new pastoral emerging – which seems to date from around the time the poets Michael Symmons Roberts and Paul Farley brought out their prose book, *Edgelands*.[4] They were doing much what Edward Thomas did (there's that man again) when he walked and cycled around England 'In Pursuit of Spring' or tracing the Icknield Way. And that alertness to pastoral is tied in with a new detoxified sense of what Englishness might mean. Grayson Perry's 2023 Channel 4 series on the subject was in the same spirit, although it was already happening in the 2010s (I think we both wish we could have included something from Andrew Motion's extraordinary long poem *Essex Clay*, but it just doesn't lend itself to excerpts), and we try to show that in our 'Divide' section. But even so short a way into this new decade there has been Zaffar Kunial's *England's Green*, Holly Hopkins's *The English Summer*, and several other very 'English' collections from Grace Nichols, Robert Selby, Gregory Leadbetter, Alison Brackenbury, Tom Sastry, John Challis and Hannah Lowe, whose *The Kids* won the last ever Costa Book of the Year. Lowe is able to say things that would have been much more controversial ten years ago, yet her work is recognisably in a line from... well, from all those Elizabethan sonneteers, I suppose. As you say, it's wonderful to find that some of the liveliest commentary comes from Black and Asian writers, although there have been decades where we weren't able to find so much material.

KG: The 70s proved to be one such decade, with very few poets of colour in this chapter.

JG: Perhaps our deliberately limiting choice of theme was the problem (there were fewer strong poems from women in that decade too), but I think our final selection for that period does work, and the theme throws up poems we might

---

4 Paul Farley and Michael Symmons Roberts, *Edgelands: Journeys into England's True Wilderness* (Jonathan Cape, 2011).

otherwise not have considered. It was a time of economic recession, but also a time for looking back, and the title has a hint of Larkin's 'Church Going' too. That's a 50s poem it would have been good to include, but his 'The Whitsun Weddings' had the right mildly ironic take on merriness for the 1960s/80s currents.

KG: Those are a nice antidote to our selections representing the 70s, which seem insistently elegiac. They aren't necessarily *nostalgic* for a lost past, because even a poet with such instincts knows that pastoral visions are patently fictional. But they are *elegiac* about the past, and sorrowful for things that cannot be recovered – medieval villages lost to coastal erosion, bucolic farmland swallowed up by industrial agriculture, disappearing branch lines, empty pubs.

JG: That's an important distinction.

KG: A recurring symbol is the ruined abbey – an English predilection that's certainly been with us a while, as far back at least as the 'gaping tombs' and 'heaps of ruin' that Pope observed in *Windsor Forest*, where 'savage howlings fill the sacred quires'. Sorry to go on about Pope again!

JG: Oh, one can never have too much Pope. He himself represents a distinctively contrarian kind of Englishness. Actually, the interest in ruins may go back even further, to that Anglo-Saxon poem about some Roman remains.

KG: A fair point. And I'm pretty sure Shakespeare wasn't thinking solely of wintry tree branches when he wrote of 'bare ruined choirs'. In any case, the despoliation of abbeys wasn't a natural process, and Pope's point in his ode to Englishness was not to elegise a romantic landscape, but to critique tyranny and expose political abuses. We certainly have a lot of poems in our collection that take a strongly political stance, don't we?

JG: From the futility of trench warfare to the consequences of mine closures, and several recent pieces about racism and social inequity. What we weren't so keen on were those noisier poems that patently had 'designs' on us, although I'm glad we allowed in a few cries of protest. At one point we had Adrian Mitchell's 'Fifteen Million Plastic Bags', but in the end the poem didn't feel English enough, whereas Adrian Henri's 'Mrs Albion' (which we opted for, as did Larkin in his Oxford anthology) is a stylistic protest, channelling the spirit of Blake. It's also amusing, and humour is at the heart of Englishness. Do you remember our conversation about Jez Butterworth's extraordinary play, *Jerusalem*? It goes to the Blakean heart of our theme quite riotously and hilariously. In fact, one of Rooster Byron's final speeches[5] – a curse on Kennet and Avon Council – is actually set out in verse: 'Any uniform which brushes a single leaf of this wood/Is cursed, and he who wears it this St George's Day,/May he not see the next'. We considered including some of it, but it doesn't work away from the stage, and the date wasn't quite right. 'Rebellion' was an especially fruitful topic for the 1960s, just as climate change is proving to be for the 2020s, although we've been quite restrained in our selections. Rebecca Watts's premature daffodils say quite enough – especially because they are daffodils, themselves a symbol of English poetry. And Philip Gross provides a powerful vision of flooded England. I remember travelling by train across the Somerset Levels he describes when they were under water, and it was apocalyptic, though very beautiful.

KG: When you introduced me to that poem I was reminded of a J.G. Ballard novel I read more than thirty years ago, *The Drowned World* – which makes me wonder whether there is ever much cross-fertilisation between science fiction and poetry. Climate change would seem to welcome that.

---

5 Played by Mark Rylance in the London and Broadway production. Quoted from Jez Butterworth, *Jerusalem* (Nick Hern Books, 2009).

JG: There's our next anthology... though I think science fiction's already been done. As a boy, the only two genres I really enjoyed (other than 'how-to' books) were poetry and science fiction, especially Arthur C. Clarke. He was a true poet, as well as a proper Englishman, and he in fact came from Somerset – as did C.H. Sisson, a poet deeply preoccupied with Englishness. Although I was brought up in London and live in Cambridgeshire, if I had to point to the heart of Englishness (I can already hear the shouts of metrical protest from Cornwall to Norfolk to Yorkshire to the Lake District) it would be in Somerset. Perhaps at St Michael's Tower on Glastonbury Tor, where 'those feet in ancient times...', and not so far from Camelot or where King Alfred burnt the cakes. Unless the rock festival is on, it might also be a good place to rest from our long journey (Glastonbury's the convergence of several important ley lines, after all). Do you think we have given our readers a taste of what they're about to read?

KG: I do hope so. I'm glad you've mentioned Sisson – a good note to end on. Sisson was probably the first poet I discovered who was so conscious and intentional in writing about Englishness. There are so many terrific lines about England one might single out, but these from 1991 seem to encapsulate our own feelings about this place:

It is a public country that I want
And so indeed it was, the world I had,
Growing from nothing to the edge of doom.
But what was in between?
The hope and love I had in fields and moors,
In hills, in waters lashing round the coast.
The coast of where? And where but you, O England,
Which name has gathered all my hopes and loves.[6]

---

6 From 'The Begging Bowl', *Collected Poems* (Carcanet, 1998).

JG: It's been a real pleasure working with you – I'm not sure how we would have done it without email and WhatsApp! Nor do we have any virtual champagne. But anyway, I now declare open this precious book, this contraflow of lines, this anthology of Englishness!

JOHN GREENING is the author of over twenty collections of poetry, most recently *The Interpretation of Owls: Selected Poems 1977–2022*. He has written studies of several major poets and edited selections of Edmund Blunden, Geoffrey Grigson, Iain Crichton Smith and U.A. Fanthorpe, along with several anthologies. His essays on poetry are collected in *Vapour Trails*. He has taught in Upper Egypt, Scotland and New Jersey, and has lived for many years with his family in Cambridgeshire.

KEVIN GARDNER is a critic, editor and Professor of English at Baylor University in Waco, Texas. He has published numerous essays on poets, from John Dryden to the present, has edited several volumes of the works of John Betjeman, and has worked on anthologies of church elegies (*Building Jerusalem*), country-house poems (*Hollow Palaces*, with John Greening) and Norfolk poetry (*Before the Dreadful Daylight Starts*, with Cameron Self).

ANGLES OF ENTRY

'This landscape is not given to forgetting.'
– U.A. Fanthorpe

2020s

Foxglove Country

Sometimes I like to hide in the word
foxgloves – in the middle of *foxgloves*.
The *xgl* is hard to say, out of the England
of its harbouring word.
Alone it becomes a small tangle,
a witch's thimble, hard-to-toll bell,
elvish door to a door. *Xgl*
a place with a locked beginning
then a snag, a *gl*
like the little Englands of my grief,
a knotted dark that locks light
in *glisten, glow, glint, gleam*
and Oberon's banks of *eglantine*
which closes in on the opening
of *Gulliver* whose shrunken *gul*
says 'rose' in my fatherland.
Meanwhile, in the motherland, the *xg*
is almost the thumb of a lost mitten,
an impossible interior, deeper than forests
and further in. And deeper inland
is the gulp, the gulf, the gap, the grip
that goes before *love*.

Zaffar Kunial

2010s

England, I loved you

in your verdant years of nostalgia, cloud-harassed
and pungent, a smokestack and chippy in every gulp
of your air. In your talking-shops, your secure
institutions, you'd drink me under every table

you'd carved from the bones of your forests,
bewitch me with your blather of moderate socialism,
the pout of your lovelies in those red-tops
on mornings of damp and desperation.

Now you abandon me to stalk your ghost towers,
shrug me off as a hedge fund jettisons acres
of brownfield, as a state outsources its grief to the lowest
bidder. I only hurt you now so you'll see me again.

David Clarke

2000s

The only thing far away

In this country, Jamaica is not quite as far
as you might think. Walking through Peckham
in London, West Moss Road in Manchester,
you pass green and yellow shops
where tie-headwomen bargain over the price
of dasheen. And beside Jamaica is Spain
selling large yellow peppers, lemon to squeeze
on to chicken. Beside Spain is Pakistan, then Egypt,
Singapore, the world… here, strangers build home
together, flood the ports with curry and papayas;
in Peckham and on Moss Road, the place smells
of more than just patty or tandoori. It smells like
Mumbai, like Castries, like Princess Street, Jamaica.
Sometimes in this country, the only thing far away
is this country.

Kei Miller

1990s

Somerset

Such gentle open slopes, such lack of drama.
A cottage there and there a tiny town
lodged in a valley, rivers overflowing
after four rainy months
but all is drying now as ubiquitous sun
points out a church spire then a gaze of windows
an almost temperate time but not quite yet.
Who knows what March may bring? Perhaps some snow
but for this Sunday late in February
Spring slips its head round corners of big clouds
and they are silvered by the raptured sun
and by me gazing. Here all good that's England
speaks in green flows of light, in church bells ringing
while afternoons are stretching out their arms
before the good day of our clocks put forward.

Elizabeth Jennings

1980s

England

Forgotten, shabby and long time abandoned
   in stubbled fur, with broken
teeth like toggles, the old gods are leaving.
   They will no longer crack the
tarmac of the language, open generous
   rivers, heal our scoured thoughts.
They will only blink, and move on, and
tomorrow no one will remember their songs

unless they rise in warning, as when
   sudden planes speed overhead
crossing the sky with harsh accelerating
   screams. You may shiver then
to hear the music of the gods leaving.
   This generation
is waiting for the boy Octavius.
   They don't like losers.
And the gods are leaving us.

Elaine Feinstein

1970s

Earthed

Not precisely, like a pylon or
A pop-up toaster, but in a general
Way, stuck in the mud.

Not budding out of it like gypsies,
Laundry lashed to a signpost, dieting on
Nettles and hedgehogs,

Not lodged in its layers like badgers,
Tuned to the runes of its home-made walls, wearing
Its shape like a skin,

Not even securely rooted, like
Tribesmen tied to the same allotment, sure of
The local buses,

But earthed for all that, in the chalky
Kent mud, thin sharp ridges between wheel-tracks, in
Surrey's wild gravel,

In serious Cotswold uplands, where
Limestone confines the verges like yellow teeth,
And trees look sideways.

Everything from the clouds downwards holds
Me in its web, like the local newspapers,
Routinely special,

Or Somerset belfries, so highly
Parochial that Gloucestershire has none, or
Literate thrushes,

Conscientiously practising the
Phrases Browning liked, the attitude Hughes noticed,
Or supermarkets

Where the cashiers' rudeness is native
To the district, though the bread's not, or gardens,
Loved more than children,

Bright with resourcefulness and smelling
Of rain. This narrow island charged with echoes
And whispers snares me.

U.A. Fanthorpe

1960s

England

for Peter Lucas, 1966

Without nostalgia who could love England?
Without a sentimental attachment to tolerance
Who could delight in this cramped corner country
In no quarter savage, where everything done well
Is touched with the melancholy of understanding.

No one leaves England enamoured,
But England remembered invites an equivocal regret.
For what traveller or exile, mesmerised by the sun
Or released by spaciousness from habitual self-denial,
Recalls without wistfulness its fine peculiarities
Or remembers with distaste its unique, vulnerable surfaces?

Summer and the shine of white leaves against thunder.
Ploughland where the wind throws the black soil loose
And horses pull clumsily as though through surf,
Or stand, hoofs clapped to the earth like bells,
Braced in their fields between churches and seagulls.
England. Cool and in bloom.
Where sky begets colours on uneasy seasons
And hills lie down patiently in the rain.

Americans like England to live in her cameo,
A dignified profile attached to a past
Understood to belong to her, like the body of a bust.

The image to the native is battered but complete,
The cracked clay flaking, reluctantly sloughed away,
Inadequately renewed on her beautiful bones.

The stinginess of England. The proliferating ugliness.
The pale boys, harmful, dissatisfied, groping for comfort
In the sodium darkness of December evenings.
Wet roofs creeping for miles along wet bricks.
Lovers urgently propping each other on the endless
Identical pavements, in the vacant light
Where the cars live, their pupilless eyes
Turned upward without envy or disapproval.

Someone must live in the stunted houses behind the stucco.
Someone must feed from the tiny sick shops.
Someone must love these babies.
                              Unbelievable
In the murk of her cottage, the eighty-year virgin
Fussing over bottles and cats; the uncharitable cold;
Light falling in squares from the frugal windows
Of public houses; schoolgirls dragging in crocodile
Through damp lanes behind the converted castle,
Querulous in the big wind. In the same wind
That gathers them, with pylons and steeples and
Gas drums, with domes and scaffolding and graveyards
And small kempt gardens by the railway, helplessly,
Recklessly, untidily into the temporary spring.

Anglers appear, umbrellas and transistors
On the paths by the silted canals; and Sunday couples
Spread like wet clothes on the bank.
Days unobtrusively seep into the nights,
Days that drew the daffodil after the crocus
And lit the rose from the embers of the hyacinth

Thrust nettle and thistle through ribs of abandoned machinery
And dye green the trunks of elaborate beeches.
Then the hills fill with gold wheat.

September. Already autumnal.
Lost days drift under the plane trees.
Leaves tangle in the gutters.
In Greenwich, in Kew, in Hampstead
The paths are dry, the ponds dazed with reflections.

Come with me. Look. The city,
Nourished by its poisons, is beautiful in them.
A pearly contamination strokes the river
As cranes ride or dissolve in it,
And the sun dissolves in the hub of its own explosion.

The seconds flare and are gone.
The season is gone that was a long time coming.
Fulfilment is like bread, and
The cornfields lie naked in the burnt shires.
But we must believe the blunt evidence of our senses
As any physicist the map of his calculations,
As any child the reasonable comfort of his mother
That the leaves are beautiful because they are dying,
That the trees are only falling asleep.

Anne Stevenson

1950s

Shipton-under-Wychwood

Under Wychwood the growth and undergrowth
contend and do not mind how things exceptional
meander into landscape. They are drenched under
and under the repetitive green at last.
Fetched into chastity are fond extravagant
and noticeable doings and undertakings
whereover all the rhythms of Cotswold ride.

Ride, and have struck an ever-receding camp
over and over again, redundant time and tenses
disposing of themselves. What horses overtake them?
and what will become of the rare and royal hunters?
Prebend plunges over Plantagenet; it is all
over, then, with the legions of Rome before
finality, split-hooved, has taken over
Shipton under the forest, concealed in summer.

Muriel Spark

1940s

An Archaeological Picnic

In this high pasturage, this Blunden time,
  With Lady's Finger, Smokewort, Lovers' Loss,
And lin-lan-lone a Tennysonian chime
    Stirring the sorrel and the gold-starred moss,
    Cool is the chancel, bright the altar cross.

Drink, Mary, drink your fizzy lemonade
    And leave the king-cups; take your grey felt hat;
Here, where the low-side window lends a shade,
    There, where the key lies underneath the mat,
    The rude forefathers of the hamlet sat.

Sweet smell of cerements and of cold wet stones,
    Hassock and cassock, paraffin and pew;
Green in a light which that sublime Burne-Jones
    White-hot and wondering from the glass-kiln drew,
    Gleams and re-gleams this Trans arcade anew.

So stand you waiting, freckled innocence!
    For me the squinch and squint and Trans arcade;
For you, where meadow grass is evidence,
    With flattened pattern, of our picnic made,
    One bottle more of fizzy lemonade.

John Betjeman

1930s

You that love England...

You that love England, who have an ear for her music,
The slow movement of clouds in benediction,
Clear arias of light thrilling over her uplands,
Over the chords of summer sustained peacefully;
Ceaseless the leaves' counterpoint in a west wind lively,
Blossom and river rippling loveliest allegro,
And the storms of wood strings brass at year's finale:
Listen. Can you not hear the entrance of a new theme?

You who go out alone, on tandem or on pillion,
Down arterial roads riding in April,
Or sad beside lakes where hill-slopes are reflected
Making fires of leaves, your high hopes fallen:
Cyclists and hikers in company, day excursionists,
Refugees from cursed towns and devastated areas;
Know you seek a new world, a saviour to establish
Long-lost kinship and restore the blood's fulfilment.

You who like peace, good sticks, happy in a small way
Watching birds or playing cricket with schoolboys,
Who pay for drinks all round, whom disaster chose not;
Yet passing derelict mills and barns roof-rent
Where despair has burnt itself out – hearts at a standstill,
Who suffer loss, aware of a lowered vitality;
We can tell you a secret, offer a tonic; only
Submit to the visiting angel, the strange new healer.

You above all who have come to the far end, victims
Of a run-down machine, who can bear it no longer;
Whether in easy chairs chafing at impotence
Or against hunger, bullies and spies preserving
The nerve for action, the spark of indignation –
Need fight in the dark no more, you know your enemies.
You shall be leaders when zero hour is signalled,
Wielders of power and welders of a new world.

C. Day Lewis

COUNTRY

'… our minds fill up
with England again, with mud.
This sludge-clump out in the North Atlantic.'
— Paul Mills

1920s

Forefathers

Here they went with smock and crook,
    Toiled in the sun, lolled in the shade,
Here they mudded out the brook
    And here their hatchet cleared the glade:
Harvest supper woke their wit,
Huntsman's moon their wooings lit.

From this church they led their brides,
    From this church themselves were led
Shoulder-high; on these waysides
    Sat to take their beer and bread.
Names are gone – what men they were
These their cottages declare.

Names are vanished, save the few
    In the old brown Bible scrawled;
These were men of pith and thew,
    Whom the city never called;
Scarce could read or hold a quill,
Built the barn, the forge, the mill.

On the green they watched their sons
    Playing till too dark to see,
As their fathers watched them once,
    As my father once watched me;
While the bat and beetle flew
On the warm air webbed with dew.

Unrecorded, unrenowned,
    Men from whom my ways begin,
Here I know you by your ground
    But I know you not within –
There is silence, there survives
Not a moment of your lives.

Like the bee that now is blown
    Honey-heavy on my hand,
From his toppling tansy-throne
    In the green tempestuous land –
I'm in clover now, nor know
Who made honey long ago.

Edmund Blunden

2020s

Daffodils push through in the mild first days of January,

prompting my colleague to say 'too soon –
they'll regret it next week when a hard frost sets in'.

And yet, for them, *early* and *late* don't mean;
they do what they do while conditions allow; and if to him

they symbolise disappointment or failure,
or the hubris of the eager,

they also show how nature deals not in *ought*
but *is* – the blip of green or yellow breaking up black

soil, perhaps not making it.

Rebecca Watts

The Knowledge

Not the knowledge chosen for the national
syllabus, nor knowledge scrawled by Mrs Smith
on the board in shaky chalk, but the knowledge
I heard my father practise, out loud after tea.

Not a knowledge of capital cities, of England's
football captains, David Beckham's scoring record,
nor any pub quiz question, but a knowledge of maps,
of London's maps in more than three dimensions.

Maps that covered the dining room, a cheap print
of *The Hay Wain*, of *Bubbles* and our photographs.
Maps he rose each day to enter, a clipboard
on his handlebars, to expand his hippocampus.

Manor House to Gibson Square; Archway
to Gloucester Gate; Penn Street to Portland Place;
Consort Road to MoD
via Peckham Rye and Westminster Bridge.

But I can't buy the wisdom that vocation
is hereditary – that sons should give their lives
to do the jobs their fathers did – instead, I learnt
not from the front, but from the back seat of his cab

ferrying decision-makers, Canary Wharf
to Portcullis House, past navvies tunnelling
the Underground, through the husk of blackout
London, and to here and now: this argument.

Taught to speak by sixteen years of answering
the register, by milk, chalk and cartridge ink,
Shakespeare and the Lord's Prayer, I raise my arm
to pay my coins, my tributes to the knowledge.

John Challis

The Only English Kid

When the debate got going on 'Englishness',
I'd pity the only English kid – poor Johnny
in his spotless Reeboks and blue Fred Perry.
He had a voice from history: *Dunno-miss*,
Yes-miss, *No-Miss* – all treacly-cockney,
rag-and-bone – and while the others claimed Poland,
Ghana, Bulgaria, and shook off England
like the wrong team's shirt, John brewed his tea

exclusively on Holloway Road. So when Aanif
mourned the George Cross banner swinging freely
like a warning from his neighbour's roof,
the subway tunnel sprayed with MUSLIM SCUM,
poor John would sit there quietly, looking guilty
for all the awful things he hadn't done.

Hannah Lowe

Greensleeves

And in the jalousied schoolhouse next door
up to her elbows in prefeminist chores –
my mother – piano hands
sunk in the belly of a fish
scales rank and translucent
freckling the cinnamon of her skin.

Or rubbing clothes across the ribbed
bridge of a scrubbing board –
the sudden O of her lost soap
the indigo of her rinsing water –
the wind-scented pleasure of harvesting
them at the clothesline later.

Now witness her, head bent
over black and white keys
surprising the ear of the creole breeze
with that Tudor melody, 'Greensleeves'.

Grace Nichols

Self-Portrait as Katharine of Aragon

I have a queen's reason
    for working my stitch-fingers to the bone
        as summer dims in green corners of England

and the radio's bedside manner blesses the air
    Wild rose, wild rose, was once my call sign
        I always loved the Spanish-speaking world

but heads and tails of silence drift into the chamber
    where I embroider time-lord clouds
        hiding sun and moon

remembering from the future that when a military plane
    finds itself in serious trouble
        the voice command switches to the feminine

But why let the future be more than my servant
    sent to do my bidding centuries from now?
        Don't tell me the future sits on the floor

the place for beggars or for one out of her wits
    The future is simply a way of hiding my heart within my own heart
        bruised and bound as it is, ruling neither Commons nor King

They say the peony or Benedictine Rose was sold
    for one hundred ounces of gold
        they say nettles also sit in the rose genus

They say the axe has been ordered from France

Penelope Shuttle

Chevening (X)

This is the real England, I say, so what do you think?
It's a place of trees; of apple, pear, cherry and plum.
In the gaps is man's history, his urge to link
with others, forge commerce, lick a thumb
to count the realm's tender or sample harvest.
The railway came, but the speed it gave the world
entangled in this bracken and broomy darkness.
Life here is at the pace a picnic blanket unfurls.
Do you want to reset your watch to the toll of here?
Our years would lengthen into a summer's evening
of wine on a lawn under bat flight. Then we'll disappear.
All that'll be left: two glasses filled with morning,
your silk scarf over one of the two empty chairs;
two lit candles in the church for us, if anyone cares.

Robert Selby

The Kingdom

I was hungry
    coming up from Kent
resorting hyther after the summer

my tent a riverbed
    seeking herbergement
some accommodation among the stone

the men coming on to you
    the taxi drivers saying here jump in no
        no you don't need no money.

I was thirsty
        languissyng in the doorway
behind the post office

the churchyard water
        so cold for washing
– what eyleth thee woman? –

and from my mouth came leaves
and from the cracks in the pavement
        came syllables.

I was a stranger
    turned half to stone
seeking releyf in severe weather

coming hyther in search of something
        oute of thys madnesse
something to inherit.

Jane Draycott

from **_Between the Islands_**

Land-islands, like their own astonishments
in the mist lake of the Levels. They're beside
themselves, like the perfectly useless remembrance
of the old, a beach suddenly vacated by the tide

before the tsunami. Brent Knoll is a square-
shouldered hunch, Glastonbury sharp and fey
as a sea-mirage, Fata Morgana, nowhere
we can hope to be. The submerged motorway

is traced by two strict shoals of glow, the red,
the white. The past, the future. Athelney's
an Isle again, as when the news-drones overhead
showed miles of flood-scape. A line of trees

wades ashore. Chafed by long drainage, the field
striped with rhynes waits, the Summerland waits,
              for the sea to return, to be healed.

Philip Gross

South and West

Outside Child's Ercall cat's paws of sleet speckled the windscreen.
Preston Gubbals was not much more than a dovecote without its doves,
but there was a rough warmth in the hewn sandstone of Ruyton-XI-Towns.
Crossing the ford at Neen Savage, the tyres sprouted wings of water.
Hopton Cangeford was morris dancing in its tassels of daffodils.
From Angelbank we looked down on squares of silver and fool's gold.

We spent the night in a layby near Hope under Dinmore,
beneath the Brutalist shadows of parked juggernauts.

Not yet lunchtime at Trumpet. The malty alcoves of the pub were deserted.
At Upper Framilode the Severn gazed out through eyelash reeds.
At Engine Common the fields had slumped into green wrinkles.
Sun pinkened the church at Acton Turville, brought Vobster out in a rash
    of daisies,
ruffled the stone heads on the gateposts at Mappowder.
We smelt the dank of wild garlic at Rime Intrinseca,
and gargoyles spat from the church tower of Toller Porcorum.
Whitchurch Canonicorum cowered under rainclouds of thatch.
Oath was shivery in the twilight, and Catcott Burtle
gathered the smoke of coal fires round it by way of a blanket.
Monksilver was a catastrophe of morning bells
as if we'd broken it. The Bronze Age yew at Ashbrittle
was a senile labyrinth, all gnarls and needled glooms.

The moor slouched on the horizon. The grass
was strawed with last year's yellow when we reached Sticklepath
and stretched our legs on its lichen-splotched slab of bridge.
At Queen Dart tussocky ponies browsed among the primroses,

and we passed Upton Hellions and Pancrasweek
in a loosening of the air, an erosion of all those accretions
of cottages, hedges, and churches, of names and stones.
Before us was simple blue, and Washaway, Stoptide, Pityme.

Matthew Francis

For Cousin John

'...land of shades!'
                    – *William Blake*

Your voice, a red and white flag,
a teatime tablecloth. *Slavery*

happened long ago, it means
nothing now. I prepare silence,

practise each time for a calm dinner

but you lift a fork, unsettle the territory.

I can't stop seeing the child
pulled from a home of hissing

and raised by our grandmother
who was endlessly scraping plates

between us. With her gone

something shifts at our table and you

keep sharpening the somewhere else
in me. No, I don't know what it's like

to live in a small military town
or how you fit where everyone is white.

Do you hold up England

by its gilt edges, best china handles?

What secretly stirs your tea? *Cousin,*
we all alone in these streets. I wish you

horses in rain and fields of broken gates.
I wish you a surprise party of sober mothers

holding a Thomas the Tank Engine birthday cake.
I wish you glistening grapes and radiated rooms.

When we stood shoulder to shoulder
at our grandmother's funeral I didn't hear you cry

but I felt your quivering, saw your red face,
the fallen flags in your eyes, Cousin, why couldn't you

let us see what you were burying? Cousin

I wish sunlight on all your fields

Raymond Antrobus

United Kingdom

Is. Your. Mother. English? demands the Welsh girl
who seems to like my tall white friend.
It is a bad moment to discover how angry I am.
Born of an English mother. You're English.

She needs an Englishman
to say English things, in an English way
so she can take his complacency
and prove herself better; thus gratified

she can flirt with my English friend
and laugh with her English colleagues
and know what burns inside her and why.
She can flame in the abstract and warm in the flesh

but not to me. If I am to be
her Englishman, she will be my white girl
ignorant and not bothered by it.
Our companions

who don't realise our quarrel is partly with them
are entertained by her passion
as she performs the ritual of her contempt
the curses and the tossed drink

which she knows
draw every eye in the bar
disciplining me with the threat
of male British violence.

Tom Sastry

[6 4]

The Morning After

1

This morning, friend, your courtesy alarms me.
I think you think I am in need of it.
Another man's honeysuckle overhangs the pavement:
You halt and beckon me through under the scent.
You smile, I smile. As I go on my way and have you behind me
I am almost certain that you bowed.
What is it, friend, fellow citizen?
I am almost certain you will never be my enemy
But your manners this ordinary morning have alarmed me.
Is there something I should know and do not know?
Like you, I am a family man.
Is the Law still my defender as it is yours?

2

Nothing personal, neighbour, but if I don't tell you
Somebody else will. Today isn't yesterday. Talking loudly
Won't do you any favours. It has become obvious
You're not our shade, are you? There are people
(Not me) will tell you your headgear
Is out of place. I know one lady
She'll tell you to your face when she uses public transport
She just wants to be with her own kind, thank you very much.
And my own father, God rest his soul
I can hear him saying he didn't round up the Mau Mau
To see the country overrun like this. Nothing personal, neighbour
I can hear him giving you his opinion
That only people born here belong here and by born here
He means way back. Don't mind me asking, neighbour
Where do you call home?

David Constantine

DIVIDE

'So we stand here, two men and a hundred years
in England between us'

— E.A. Markham

1930s

Birmingham

Smoke from the train-gulf hid by hoardings blunders upward, the brakes of cars
Pipe as the policeman pivoting round raises his flat hand, bars
With his figure of a monolith Pharaoh the queue of fidgety machines
(Chromium dogs on the bonnet, faces behind the triplex screens).
Behind him the streets run away between the proud glass of shops,
Cubical scent-bottles artificial legs arctic foxes and electric mops,
But beyond this centre the slumward vista thins like a diagram:
There, unvisited, are Vulcan's forges who doesn't care a tinker's damn.

Splayed outwards through the suburbs houses, houses for rest
Seducingly rigged by the builder, half-timbered houses with lips pressed
So tightly and eyes staring at the traffic through bleary haws
And only a six-inch grip of the racing earth in their concrete claws;
In these houses men as in a dream pursue the Platonic Forms
With wireless and cairn terriers and gadgets approximating to the fickle norms
And endeavour to find God and score one over the neighbour
By climbing tentatively upward on jerry-built beauty and sweated labour.

The lunch hour: the shops empty, the shopgirls' faces relax
Diaphanous as green glass, empty as old almanacs
As incoherent with ticketed gewgaws tiered behind their heads
As the Burne-Jones windows in St Philip's broken by crawling leads;
Insipid colour, patches of emotion, Saturday thrills
(This theatre is sprayed with 'June') – the gutter take our old playbills,
Next weekend it is likely in the heart's funfair we shall pull
Strong enough on the handle to get back our money; or at any rate it is possible.

On shining lines the trams like vast sarcophagi move
Into the sky, plum after sunset, merging to duck's egg, barred with mauve
Zeppelin clouds, and Pentecost-like the cars' headlights bud
Out from sideroads and the traffic signals, crème de menthe or bull's blood,
Tell one to stop, the engine gently breathing, or to go on
To where like black pipes of organs in the frayed and fading zone
Of the West the factory chimneys on sullen sentry will all night wait
To call, in the harsh morning, sleep-stupid faces through the daily gate.

Louis MacNeice

2010s

Another Country

'Get there if you can.'
  – *Auden*

Scattered comrades, now remember: someone stole the staffroom tin
Where we collected for the miners, for the strike they couldn't win,

Someone stole a tenner, tops, and then went smirkingly away.
Whoever did it, we have wished you thirsty evil to this day:

You stand for everything there was to loathe about the South –
The avarice, the snobbery, the ever-sneering mouth,

The lack of solidarity with any cause but *me*,
The certainty that what you were was what the world should be.

The North? Another country. No one you knew ever went.
(Betteshanger, Snowdown, Tilmanstone: where were they? In Kent.)

'People' tell us nowadays these views are terribly unfair,
But these forgiving 'people' aren't the 'people' who were there.

Meanwhile your greying children smile and shrug: *That's history.*
So what's the point of these laments for how things used to be?

Whenever someone sagely says it's time to draw a line,
We may infer that they've extracted all the silver from the mine.

Where all year long the battle raged, there's 'landscape' and a plaque,
But though you bury stuff forever, It keeps on coming back:

Here then lie the casualties of one more English Civil War,
That someone, sometime – you, perhaps – will have to answer for.

Sean O'Brien

Driving through the Pit Town

There's not much round here now, you say,
just huddled brick or pebbledash terraces,
and tiny new-builds where the pitheads were.

Bare hills fly up beyond the town you left,
with clasps of scree, caps of sodden green,
pitched above the neat slate pitches

but your eyes stay on the road. The side streets jut
left and right, so many of them, like ribs.
You jab a finger: *We lived up top of that one.*

Then – surprise – a pale sun picks at a slit
in the paper sky. Yellow slaps down
momently and slides along the valley,

and the half-a-pit-wheel trenched in the roundabout
shimmers, red as flesh. We won't stop here
and most of the shops – Kebabland, USA Nail's,

Milan Fashions – are shut or boarded anyway.
The four lads pincering fags outside the Co-op,
gobbing and shoving, repulse for what they are.

It's no use knowing better, more, you say.
And in blue spray paint, the back of the village sign
cries DING DONG!! like we're waiting at a door.

                                          2013

Rory Waterman

Homing

For years you kept your accent
in a box beneath the bed,
the lock rusted shut by hours of elocution
how now brown cow
the teacher's ruler across your legs.

We heard it escape sometimes,
a guttural *uh* on the phone to your sister,
saft or *blart* to a taxi driver
unpacking your bags from his boot,
I loved its thick drawl, *g*'s that rang.

Clearing your house, the only thing
I wanted was that box, jemmied open
to let years of lost words spill out —
bibble, fittle, tay, wum,
vowels ferrous as nails, consonants

you could lick the coal from.
I wanted to swallow them all: the pits,
railways, factories thunking and clanging
the night shift, the red brick
back-to-back you were born in.

I wanted to forge your voice
in my mouth, a blacksmith's furnace;
shout it from the roofs,
send your words, like pigeons,
fluttering for home.

Liz Berry

Bridge

What makes a bridge beautiful is its curve,
arching above an image of itself:
doubles, one sharp and one mysterious,
two versions of a tale in fact and myth.
My grandfather's is fact. The Chinese Bridge
that spans the Great Ouse at Godmanchester,
from the flat ground we call the Boys' School Hill
to the Rec, is his – it sprang from his hand.
When Brudenell's tendered for it, no one thought
to find out if the plans from years before
were still around; my grandfather was left
to take the old bridge down and measure up,
piecing the new together on the grass
against the old bones like a giant kit.
A length of rope from pier to pier and from
the apex to the average river height
was their geometry – he and his mate,
plumbing it down to catch the arch's depth.
The distance was exactly seven feet,
with six more inches for the joints to drop,
though in the end the joints were tight and good
and didn't fall an eighth and so the bridge
flexed up six inches prouder than it should
or so one local pundit said who couldn't
himself have set a plank across a ditch.
At the official opening the Mayor
and Corporation crossed in due process
and someone made a speech and people clapped.
The men who built the bridge stood at the back.
Nobody thought a workman worth the time
to write an invitation. Fair enough:

they took a half-hour off. The plans turned up
eventually, and proved by chance the arch
was seven-feet-six above the water-top.
So there it was, perfect, exact, an arc
pure as a swan's neck, its white reflection
shifting and slipping in a weedy web.
And in the undertow the worlds invert:
in that refracted underwater land
what's yours is what your making hands have touched
and turned and worked and struggled with in thought.
One day you may look down and watch them cross –
the broken shining people in a net
of light, fragmented, lambent, as the sun
burns through an after-image of a bridge.
About their limbs the fish will glide and glint.
And who shall say whose foot is first, whose last?

Stuart Henson

Migration

When I see a hand first raised, then placed
on the heart, the head tilted towards the heart,

a greeting exchanged between a pedestrian
and a passing bus driver; when I see a woman

seated at a bus stop wave to a woman passenger
sitting behind me and, picturing them still,

look straight into trees, tears spring to my eyes
even though we're stopped at Elephant & Castle.

All one way blows the wind in the trees but
which is the way to a staging post between

the Khalvatis now, scattered in the diaspora,
and our very first forebears who struck camp,

loaded their beasts, set their caravans against
a skyline, wind whipping the horses' manes,

the fringes of their saddlecloths and shawls,
and moved as a whole tribe together?

Mimi Khalvati

Cricket

Another one of those Pyrrhic experiences. Call it
an ex*pyrrh*ience. A day at Lord's, mostly rain,
one of those long-drawn-out draws so perplexing to Americans.

Nothing riding on the game, two mid-table counties
at the end of a disappointing season, no local rivalry or anything like that,
very few people there, the game itself going nowhere slowly

on its last morning. The deadest of dead rubbers.
Papa had his beer, but you two must have wondered what you'd done wrong.
Did I say it was raining, and the forecast was for more rain?

Riveting. A way, at best, for the English
to read their newspapers out of doors, and get vaguely shirty
or hot under the collar about something. The paper, maybe, or the rain.

Occasionally lifting their eyes to watch the groundsmen at their antics –
not just hope over experience but hope over certain knowledge.
It was like staying to watch your horse lose.

And yet there was some residual sense of good fortune to be there,
perhaps it was the fresh air or being safely out of range of conversation
or the infinitesimal prospect of infinitesimal entertainment.

One groundsman – the picador – mounted on a tractor,
others on foot, like an army of clowns, with buckets and besoms.
The tractor was towing a rope across the outfield to dry it –

we saw the water spray up, almost in slow motion –
as from newly cut hair. The old rope was so endearingly *vieux jeu*.
It approached a pile of sawdust – two failing styles of drying –

and one of the groundsmen put out his foot to casually flick it over,
as sporting a gesture as we expected to see all day
in terms of finesse, economy of movement, timing.

He missed, and instead the rope sliced right through the sawdust pile,
and flattened it. A malicious laugh, widely dispersed and yet
    unexpectedly hearty,
went up on all sides of the ground. Soft knocks that school a lifetime
    – no?

Michael Hofmann

Walk with Me

I walk through Brixton with a young man
in screw-faced street mode,
and I tell him it's okay to relax.
His temptations course through his blood.
He calls me witness, he calls me bookish.
We walk avoiding certain streets,
Loughborough, the railway. We both know why.

I tell him that under these very streets we walk,
deep beneath the concrete, beneath the tarmac,
beneath the rubble, the dirt, and the rock,
there is a river flowing called Effra.
A black and powerful river coursing without light.
That one hundred and fifty years ago
royalty would sail down this river
in their best finery into Brixton
never thinking about crack, never thinking about cafés.

But every now and then
these towerblocks act like speakers
and the calming sound of a pure, flowing river
can be heard throughout Brixton's streets.
I tell him that even though the river calls,
things have moved on here.
Brixton is not its history,
and neither should we be
though we hear the call of the past.

Roger Robinson

Etcetera

Great Britain impoverished to post-war prosperity:
everyone working, but nobody earning and nothing
to buy. Capital needed labour for its unsocial
dirty work, but the natives wouldn't shift or shovel shit.

Jamaica & sub-continent took up the White Man's Burdens.
Race-rioting Teds, half-devil and half-child; Mosley,
that infantile Satan, master of puppets. Elite psychology
of fascism: malleable masses dependably deployable in the service
of their masters, to know – and keep – their place. *Send them back!*

Roman foreboding largely unwarranted. It naturalised
to jargon – multi-cultural, multi-ethnic, multi-faith –
and reality on the ground, common humanity working
its warmcockle nostrums. People simply got used to it,
to each other, cordially embracing, ignoring or hating.
A provisional peace of geniality and ghettos,
subject to periodic eruption. I was born to this.
The young know nothing else. This is England.

Steve Ely

Kerrie

At a charity event on a village green
in the Cambridgeshire countryside:
toddlers on a bouncy-castle, all running
and falling and caterwauling,
their mothers already at a makeshift bar –
it's seven o'clock somewhere – buying Pimm's
by the pitcher. Then the school bully seated
at the British Legion cake-stand, still pouty
and freckle-faced, dabbing the corners
of her baby's milky mouth with the cotton-
softness reserved for a person who has never
slammed anyone's head against a locker.

Elisabeth Sennitt Clough

The Walled Garden

Across the road, the girls quit school in threes
and fours, tripping off at speed to stations

or familiar cars, their silhouettes, slung
with shoulder bags and hockey sticks, like mules.

Remember, says the afternoon; the shut
door shudders brassily beneath my hand.

It is already dark, or darkening –
that sky above the dimming terraced rows

goes far beyond a child's imagining.
I tread along the backstreet where the cabs

cut through behind the luminous science labs –
their sills of spider plants in yoghurt pots

among the outsize glassware cylinders
like pygmies contemplating monoliths.

You cannot walk the other side because
the walled garden meets the road direct

in pools of spangled tarmac after rain;
the open gutter choking up with leaves.

As though to listen, the colossal trees
lean out into the tungsten-haloed street.

I meet another on the road – this snail's
slow ribbon turns the asphalt into gold.

Sarah Howe

Stamping Grounds (Earlier)

'(for their days were long before the days of photographs), my first
fancies regarding what they were like, were unreasonably derived
from their tombstones. The shape of the letters…'

— *Charles Dickens,* Great Expectations

1

My English grandfather, whose name in my father's language
means 'land', the earliest ground I ever held was yours.
I can see it leave my fist, beneath a sleeve
of my first school blazer. The only other 'dust to dust' earth I've let go –
further west, twenty years on – was for Mum, who you raised
behind the counter of the Polesworth post office, on Bridge
Street; your home turf, handed down from your mother,
a sub-postmistress, who'd tap messages in Morse
and who I'd discover, years after, yards away
from that opening grave I'd stood at. And thereabouts
I'd find her parents – the Deemings – and theirs,
and theirs, and theirs, at a handful of plots, marked
and unmarked, in the grounds that ring the Abbey at Polesworth.
And later I'd hear that John Donne stayed in this same village,
in the same consecrated acre, even punning on the Earth's poles
as he rode out, mouthing lines to the East, one Good Friday
across a fading forest of Arden towards the borderlands
of the Marches – where Mum would be buried –
in days when messages went on the hoof, and by hand.

In these quickened times
I can't help reading POST OFFICE with the POST
first meaning 'after'; post-natal, postscript, postponed...
In the blank, unsorted space between other thoughts –
of Mum delaying, forever, giving you a headstone for dates
and names to cut; how, so far, I've done the same
all these years after you, and Mum, had passed on;
and how Donne's journey spanned these two graves –
something small has occurred to me. Picturing when
I first stood with Mum, as your coffin was draped with that flag
from your RAF days, I imagined a lichened slab, ivied impossibly
in later time. And there, behind the moss on *Stanley Arthur Evetts*,
the S— A— E— that surely raised a comment
in passing as you signed off, in shorthand, some parcel
across the counter. To you both
it must have been as familiar as old weather in the sky
but those letters I'd never seen
are news to me – news as full as the empty tomb
to Magdalene, when the rock rolled away –
a kind of ground, or earth
I'd only picked up on today.

Zaffar Kunial

White Cliffs

Worth their salt, England's white cliffs;
a glittering breastplate
Caesar saw from his ship;
the sea's gift to the land,
where samphire pickers hung from their long ropes,
gathering, under a gull-glad sky,
in Shakespeare's mind's eye; astonishing
in Arnold's glimmering verse;
marvellous geology, geography;
to time, deference; war, defence;
first view or last of here, home,
in painting, poem, play, in song;
something fair and strong implied in chalk,
what we might wish ourselves.

Carol Ann Duffy

KEEP CALM

'Come here my love, and sit by me,
We'll love each other until tea.
You'll keep my heart and body warm
While I will try to shield from harm
As much of you as I can hold –
I think the tea is growing cold.'

– *Ruth Silcock*

1940s

Still Falls the Rain

The Raids, 1940. Night and Dawn

Still falls the Rain –
Dark as the world of man, black as our loss –
Blind as the nineteen hundred and forty nails
Upon the Cross.

Still falls the Rain
With a sound like the pulse of the heart that is changed to the
    hammer-beat
In the Potter's Field, and the sound of the impious feet

On the Tomb:
        Still falls the Rain
In the Field of Blood where the small hopes breed and the human brain
Nurtures its greed, that worm with the brow of Cain.

Still falls the Rain
At the feet of the Starved Man hung upon the Cross.
Christ that each day, each night, nails there, have mercy on us –
On Dives and on Lazarus:
Under the Rain the sore and the gold are as one.

Still falls the Rain –
Still falls the Blood from the Starved Man's wounded Side:
He bears in His Heart all wounds – those of the light that died,
The last faint spark
In the self-murdered heart, the wounds of the sad uncomprehending dark,

The wounds of the baited bear –
The blind and weeping bear whom the keepers beat
On his helpless flesh… the tears of the hunted hare.

Still falls the Rain –
Then – O Ile leape up to my God: who pulles me doune –
See, see where Christ's blood streames in the firmament:
It flows from the Brow we nailed upon the tree
Deep to the dying, to the thirsting heart
That holds the fires of the world – dark-smirched with pain
As Caesar's laurel crown.

Then sounds the voice of One who like the heart of man
Was once a child who among beasts has lain –
'Still do I love, still shed my innocent light, my Blood, for thee.'

Edith Sitwell

2000s

All Possibilities

My dead father, who never knew what hit him,
is taking his evening walk through the village.
My brother and I tag along too, kicking stones
at a respectful distance, also our Norfolk terrier,
and my mother in her hospital bed: that rasp-rasp
will be her iron wheels as they disturb the gravel.

His mood is bad. The war ended again this morning
and although he still won, it no longer feels that way.
How come the new town simmering on the horizon?
How come the blank faces and no one remembering
his name? The final straw arrives with the old park,
now a golf course, where his grandparents used to live.

With one hand he is already holding his walking stick
the wrong way round, ready to swing at buttercups;
with the other he shades his eyes and tries to make out
who is playing, and who are the ghosts of his ancestors.
They advance steadily through the twilight and threaten
to circle him, wearing the bright diamond sweaters.

'Fore!' he is shouting, to cover all possibilities. 'Fore!'

Andrew Motion

The Thames Never Breathes

out any more, only ever sucks
at the sea, its mouth to the east
thirstier by the week. I have walked
to the source. It is nothing
but a patch of stones, a tiny spring,
some well-fed cows. Yesterday,
the stones were bright with marsh
marigolds, cows moved to
higher ground. I can count
to one hundred under water.

Katrina Naomi

A Map of Rochdale

We are not London or Germany.
The war barely touched us here. I am drained
by allusions and distances, signs to twin towns
hundreds of miles away, replicas of clock towers,
the clone shop confusion of every town high street.

Let us make our own map of the sprawl,
its life and ours, a bit unseemly and tough,
filled with early sexual adventures
stemming from boredom and flesh. Politics
grown from isolation and inverted snobbery.

We'll rename the streets after their real stories,
Smack Head Valley. Skinhead Avenue,
Race Riot Street. Touch Me There Road.
Drug Deal Walk. First Kiss Gardens.
Pissed-up Lane. Possibility Fields.

John Siddique

Dead End

Aching to find what is left of old England I stray
off the helltrack of motorways
to a Roman road with a new but apt name –
'Red Route'; now bloodied with accidents,
marked by flowers, grazed posts and stripped tyres.
Prone to seek what still could be sacred –
maybe signed, 'Holy Well', or after a saint –
I turn off this too. Once-gracious farmland
put to carcinogens might still show – yes, it does:
an England earlier veiled by the flash of cars.
Around a village of worn stone
gnawing sheep for centuries sculpt
a fabric of herbs and flowers
and bells command in a golden tower
that strikes a blue sky astir with birds.
I park in a dead end and I join
the sublimely forgetful, or so they seem,
ushered to their cosy services.
Within is a sense of voices almost heard,
and shafts of honey light
divide shadows and catch faded pictures
whose solemn icons have lost their meaning,
and only the Devil laughs.

All revives the yearning
that lures us back to a seeming peace –
though spilled blood, cruelty and war
will have marked here more.
What does it give us, the past?
Massage for our sentiments?
Fantasies to match the cast of our minds?

Props for an England of privilege and habit
expressed so softly that we hardly notice
(snobbery masked as humility) until some thrust
out of Ireland, Africa or our appalled North says,
we've had enough, wake from your daze?

Or is it a vast of thinned-out air
where the spirit hovers
and maybe greets with surprise
a new friend caught in a forgotten place;
John Taverner in Boston, say;
a spirit closer than most that are now here,
communicating, out of nowhere, something?

Glyn Hughes

Hung

We are suspended above the street,
twelve floors up, nine clouds down,
north of the river, south of peace.
Beneath our feet the city is blossoming
with wet umbrellas on living stalks,
men and women on business
less concrete than poppies.

We float without time.
The whole of London is our present,
sent to us in battered envelopes
postmarked Srinagar, Ramallah, Grozny.
Torn free, the pieces tumble out,
shreds of something we have known
ever since we read the name
in other countries, in second-hand books.
Familiar street signs,
parts of jigsawed parks
posted, received, patched together at last.

The world set out below us grows
closer every day. This has become
our neighbourhood,
these our neighbours.

Those feet
we hear hurrying over
Southwark bridge or down a Kabul street
belong to people we know

people we expect to meet.

Imtiaz Dharker

Going Places

Doze on a haycock, you wake to what's occurred –
the flood has taken you.
Bobbing beneath arches, swept down weirs
you find yourself in England still,
Wansford-in-England or wherever
a tale once told is a name given.

A burglar alarm the neighbourhood has heard
is indispensable.
The bridge alone preserves amenities –
oncoming cars may claim the precedence
and delay your approach to a spirelet's
modest guardianship of warriors and kings,

but this ancient coach-road's occupation's over
and mine with it.
Behaviour and assets on-approval-please
were not enough: nothing is
ever, it would seem
old age is an abandoned market place.

These weighty grey-gold limestone stanchions
may secrete new customers –
the magnetic hostelry Olde England's plagued
with a conference from the county business park
and on local TV Gemma
guesses correctly and will receive a prize,

while I nod off like Barnaby, sloshed on a ploughman's lunch
to dream of haycocks
blown away. Where can I be?

Whose are these faces? Everything is elsewhere
beside the ceaseless slash
and thrust of eager bypass traffic, going places.

Glen Cavaliero

The Road

*Travellers leaving their horses overnight at the prehistoric burial site of
Wayland's Smithy believed they would find them newly shod by morning.*

Full once of the kind of folk you might well hope
to meet, this field or street's deserted, empty
even of footprints. Of the ancient shoe by the side
of the road, of the articles dropped and of the suitcases
no sign or symbol at all. More than the question of oaks
or beeches, their age or purpose, is the wordless army
of fence posts, the deliberate mist which gathers at night,
frost's covert displacing of stones from the rockface.

And now here's this turn in the weather: the storms
which arrive like a shipwreck from nowhere, the consequent wait
in a lifeboat, tipped like a cup to the lip of the tide,
the stowaways eyeing their feet, spectral and blue with
the distance they've travelled, shoeless and hopeful, from home.
All the locals are able to say is that promises made
have yet to be kept, that firing starts around midnight
and travellers passing will sometimes make offerings or music.

Jane Draycott

English Zen

A warm wind drifts down the Isel valley,
carting off seedheads, tugging my arm
with its luscious pastoral sympathy
and the cuckoo's comical 'Here I am'.
Plaintive too, a call that absorbs
distance into its heart like rain
so we've two valleys to walk towards,
a probable English Zen

where the eyelets of our walking boots
are furred with green for ever and ever
and minds are rattled under their slates
by the ram-stam of the river.
It drags at the meadow's root and footing.
A staff of life. Old snake in the grass.
The back-flick hums a perfect nothing
as the fisherman makes his cast.

William Scammell

Bollockshire

You've zoomed through it often enough
on the long grind north, the grim dash south −
    why not take a break?
    Slip off the motorway
at any one of ten tangled junctions
and poke your nose, without compunction,
    into the unknown.
    Get systematically lost.
At the first absence of a signpost,
opt for the least promising lane,
    or cut into the truck traffic
    along some plain,
perimeter-fence-lined stretch of blacktop
heading nowhere obvious.
    Open your mind
    to the jarring yellow
of that hillside rape crop, the grim Norse green
of that fir plantation, where every tree
    steps forward to greet you
    with the same zombie gesture
of exclamation, the last-ditch brown of −
what could it be? Something to do with pigs?
    Row on row
    of miniature Nissen huts
laid out like a new speculative estate
in acres of glistening mud, behind an electronic gate…
    But don't stop now.
    Press on,
undistracted by the lush hedgerows
(of which there are none)

or the silence of the songbirds.
Other counties

can match these. It's the essence of Bollockshire
you're after: its secrets, its blessings and bounties.
So keep driving,
past sly-windowed farms,
lying there with hoards of costly machinery
in their arms, like toys they won't share;
past Bald Oak Hill,
down the more shaded side of which
the Bollockshire Hunt has scuffled
many a morning to its kill;
past St Boldric's church,
with the slant steeple,
which Cromwell's lads once briefly visited,
leaving behind them saints re-martyred,
the Virgin without her head;
past Bewlake Manor's
dinky Gothic gatehouse, now the weekend habitat
of London media or money people;
past the isolated
Bulldog pub,
with its choice of scrumpies, microwave grub,
bouncy castle and back-room badger fights –
past all that,
until, if you are lucky,
you hit the famous ring road. Thrown down
decades ago, like a gigantic concrete garland
around the county town,
riddled and plugged
by the random dentistry of maintenance work
and chock-a-block with contraflow,
it must, you feel,
be visible from the moon.

One road sign hides another. There are orange cones
galore. Each cultivated roundabout island
            is, if possible, more off-key
            than the one before.
But don't stick here all afternoon:
Blokeston itself has to be seen,
            via the brick maze
            of its by-gone industrial outskirts.
This is where Silas Balk invented his machine
for putting a true, tight twist in string,
            where they once supplied the world
            with all it needed
of bicycle saddles and cigarette papers,
where cough syrup was king.
            Round the corner,
            just when you least expect,
there's Blokeston FC, home of 'The Blockers',
and Blokeston Prison, by the same no-frills architect.
            Unmissable from any position,
            the Bulwark Brewery
stands up in a haze of its own malty vapours,
which even today's counterwafts of Tandoori
            cannot contest.
            Now, turn east or west,
and you'll find yourself on a traffic planner's
one-way inward spiral, passing at speed
            through older and older
            parts of town –
the impeccable Georgian manners
of Beauclerc Square, built on slave-trade money;
            bad Bishop Bloggs's school;
            the crossroads where
the Billhook Martyrs were tortured and burned –
until you reach the river Bleak.

Squeeze, if you can,
over the Black Bridge,
then park and pay – assuming this isn't the week
of the Billycock Fair, or Boiled Egg Day,
when they elect the Town Fool.
From here, it's a short step
to the Bailiwick Hall Museum and Arts Centre.
As you enter, ignore the display
of tankards and manacles, the pickled head
of England's Wisest Woman;
ask, instead, for the Bloke Stone.
Surprisingly small, round, featureless,
pumice-grey,
there it sits, dimly lit,
behind toughened glass, in a room of its own.
Be sure to see it, if you've a taste
for this sort of primitive conundrum.
Most visitors pass
and won't even leave their vehicles,
keen by this time to make haste
back to the life they know,
and to put more motorway under them.

Christopher Reid

Bam Chi Chi La La:
London, 1969

I

Calm as a Coromantyn warrior baring his chest
to the branding iron, this man was standing outside
a corner Lyons in January, wearing a thin floral shirt.
One helluvabitch cold tore at the hibiscus over his heart.
So he unbuttoned button after button until almost
barechested, he stood calm as a Coromantyn warrior
giving it up dry-eyed to the white hot branding iron.

II

In Jamaica she was a teacher. Here, she is charwoman
at night in the West End. She eats a cold midnight meal
carried from home and is careful to expunge her spice
trail with Dettol. She sings 'Jerusalem' to herself and
recites the Romantic poets as she mops hallways and
scours toilets, dreaming the while of her retirement
mansion in Mandeville she is building brick by brick.

Lorna Goodison

Parade's End

Dad parked our Granada, champagne-gold
by our superstore on Blackstock Road,
my brother's eyes scanning the men
who scraped the pavement frost to the dole,
one 'got on his bike' over the hill
or the few who warmed us a thumbs-up
for the polished recovery of our re-sprayed car.

Council mums at our meat display
nestled against a pane with white trays
swilling kidneys, liver and a sandy block
of corned beef, loud enough about the way
darkies from down south *Come op ta*
Yorksha, mekkin claaims on aut theh can
befoh buggrin off in theh flash caahs!

At nine, we left the emptied till open,
clicked the dials of the safe. Bolted
two metal bars across the back door
(with a new lock). Spread trolleys
at ends of the darkened aisles. Then we pressed
the code for the caged alarm and rushed
the precinct to check it was throbbing red.

Thundering down the graffiti of shutters
against the valley of high-rise flats.
Ready for the getaway to our cul-de-sac'd
semi-detached, until we stood stock-still:
watching the car-skin pucker, bubbling smarts
of acid. In the unstoppable pub-roar
from the John O'Gaunt across the forecourt,

we returned up to the shop, lifted a shutter,
queued at the sink, walked down again.
Three of us, each carrying pans of cold water.
Then we swept away the bonnet-leaves
from gold to the brown of our former colour.

Daljit Nagra

Scene at a Conference

The kindliness of the English: a paper presented
to the ethnicity conference in Dublin in
2004. The thesis commented

on their slow smiles in a suburban garden
in North London in the early 60s. It cited
a middle-aged hand fingering a pattern

of glossy box-hedge leaves. On being invited
to elaborate, the writer mentioned the old
woman who shyly brought cups of tea to benighted

refugees waiting for a bus one particularly cold
December; three boys in a playground taking
pity on a loner in the doorway who would unfold

an incomprehensible story to them, shaking
with tears; WVS squadrons, patient
bureaucrats at office desks, their heads aching

with figures, and surprisingly efficient
bands of secretaries holding open lines,
all comprehending, almost omniscient.

The constancy of kindliness. The signs
of kindliness on rain-soaked building sites,
in electric sub-stations and down coal mines.

The forms of kindliness: terrible nights
of diffidence in front rooms, quiet
interminable minutes interrupted by flights

of fancy, the unspoken etiquette
of the lower-middle-class tea party; loss
and the coping with; desire within set

limits: all this equated with kindliness.
Warm beer and cricket, mumbled someone
at the back, who had already given his address.

And it was true, there was considerably more fun
at the Gael end of things, at the high table:
charm, invention, a recently fired gun.

George Szirtes

ALL CHANGE

'Between the empty cans and dustbin lids,
Between the eyes of cats and tramps,
Incubated drunks mumbling incomprehensible bids,
Crashed out under yellow water lamps.
This is England, I said, on a soap box in the street.'

— *Lemn Sissay*

1950s

Middlesex

Gaily into Ruislip Gardens
   Runs the red electric train,
With a thousand Ta's and Pardon's
   Daintily alights Elaine;
Hurries down the concrete station
With a frown of concentration,
Out into the outskirt's edges
Where a few surviving hedges
Keep alive our lost Elysium – rural Middlesex again.

Well cut Windsmoor flapping lightly,
   Jacqmar scarf of mauve and green
Hiding hair which, Friday nightly,
   Delicately drowns in Drene;
Fair Elaine the bobby-soxer,
Fresh-complexioned with Innoxa,
Gains the garden – father's hobby –
Hangs her Windsmoor in the lobby,
Settles down to sandwich supper and the television screen.

Gentle Brent, I used to know you
   Wandering Wembley-wards at will,
Now what change your waters show you
   In the meadowlands you fill!
Recollect the elm trees misty
And the footpaths climbing twisty
Under cedar-shaded palings,
Low laburnum-leaned-on railings
Out of Northolt on and upward to the heights of Harrow hill.

Parish of enormous hayfields
  Perivale stood all alone,
And from Greenford scent of mayfields
  Most enticingly was blown
Over market gardens tidy,
Taverns for the *bona fide*,
Cockney singers, cockney shooters,
Murray Poshes, Lupin Pooters,
Long in Kensal Green and Highgate silent under soot and stone.

John Betjeman

1990s

A Major Road for Romney Marsh

It is a kingdom, a continent.
Nowhere is like it.
                    (Ripe for development)

It is salt, solitude, strangeness.
It is ditches, and windcurled sheep.
It is sky over sky after sky.

                    (It wants hard shoulders, Happy Eaters,
                    Heavy breathing of HGVs)

It is obstinate hermit trees.
It is small, truculent churches
Huddling under the gale force.

                    (It wants WCs, Kwiksaves,
                    Artics, Ind Ests, Jnctns)

It is the Military Canal
Minding its peaceable business,
Between the Levels and the Marsh.

                    (It wants *investing in roads*,
                    Sgns syng T'DEN, F'STONE, C'BURY)

It is itself, and different.
                    (Nt fr lng. Nt fr lng.)

U.A. Fanthorpe

A View from Stansted

A cold vision is settling into place: barbed
certainties that mark red in the balance sheet
the questioner, the immigrant, the reflective;
it crushes discourse beneath its monologue
and proves dreams pathology; sees us scrabbling
on a dying planet and sneers Why not? Colonised
England wakes to find itself facing itself
in the rigid lines of winners and losers.
Its vaunting irony, its booted curled-lip
humour, its scything realism that takes
every thought at the knee, its trip-wire horror
of all touch except tickle and rape, are coming
home to us down the inevitable lanes
to claim their birthright and to wear our face.

Brian Jones

Home

These days whenever I stay away too long,
anything I happen to clap eyes on,
(that red telephone box) somehow makes me
miss here more than anything I can name.

My heart performs a jazzy drum solo
when the crow's feet on the 747
scrape down at Heathrow. HM Customs…
I resign to the usual inquisition,

telling me with Surrey loam caked
on the tongue, home is always elsewhere.
I take it like an English middleweight
with a questionable chin, knowing

my passport photo's too open-faced,
haircut wrong (an afro) for the decade;
the stamp, British Citizen not bold enough
for my liking and too much for theirs.

The cockney cab driver begins chirpily
but can't or won't steer clear of race,
so rounds on Asians. I lock eyes with him
in the rearview when I say I live with one.

He settles at the wheel grudgingly,
in a huffed silence. Cha! Drive man!
I have legal tender burning in my pocket
to move on, like a cross in Transylvania.

At my front door, why doesn't the lock
recognise me and budge? I give an extra
twist and fall forward over the threshold
piled with the felicitations of junk mail,

into a cool reception in the hall.
Grey light and close skies I love you.
Chokey streets, roundabouts and streetlamps
with tyres chucked round them, I love you.

Police officer, your boots need re-heeling.
Robin Redbreast, special request – a burst
of song so the worm can wind to the surface.
We must all sing for our suppers or else.

Fred D'Aguiar

Satellite

A dish points outwards from our outside wall
to what we cannot see: stars that know all
more clearly than these nightly Movie Greats
the fate of earthen empires. The new estates
that blinker us from crystal ballroom spaces,
haul us on in their fibre-optic traces,
plough constellations; with a flash of shares
u-turning, leave the Great and Little Bears
extinct and gilt-edged bars of progress furrowed
down the land's face. All that we have is borrowed:
museums full of stuffed trophies slowly
decaying. Territories that tick. Holy
marbles seeming to breathe. Even these words I
mix to purity, and this island time
we live on, living off serials, then soap,
and lastly just news – that shooting green hope
our parents plotted as the world turned red,
not with sunset, nor shame, but foreign dead.
We wait, hungry, now we have cleaned the Great
from Britain, scraped it out, shrunk it, wait
for a force beyond this uttermost storey
of our high rise, a column whose glory
will be to have relieved us of our fame,
of all that mafficking, cheering of a name
picked blind from a skull and nailed to the sky.
The dish receives its message from on high
in beams that swaddle the earth, in curves
of parabolic reckoning, then serves
us word made flesh: chained bare Salome sprawled
before us, while Civilisation's bald
chronicler slots between those repeats of Wars
for King and Country networked in the stars.

John Greening

Tudor Garden,
Southampton

We are plotting a tunnel of tree poles
to rose-terraces and fishpond.
Our herb-hedge mars the names. Hyssop,
dwarf sage, properly in adjunct.
Enlarging shadows fold our home
in protection at All Hallows Eve.

The jagged lightning ash spoils things.
It nudges at endings. My father
tells a boy to shore it down.
I tend a knot of green rainbows.
Homegrowing emblems clinch us
to Court. To the Colonies. Each Spring

shouts out our trust in constellation.
We're part of things. We've heard
of voyages of ambush, new plants from abroad.
Rose-wine lips our stone jugs in the bower.
I clip and tie. My father takes drink
with the men who remain.

In the harbour you can almost see,
the greyed fleet slinks and nods.
I've seen it other years: the burnt boys
carried last, when everyone's gone.
My brother won't come. From this stone
you hear the flags snap on the wind.

My mother talks to plants, tells me
their names, not writ down,
and conserves medicine upon our hurts.
At night my father bends upon new maps,
while she traps fleas in tubes
of china clay, sewn in under my skirts.

Ruth Padel

About Benwell

Perhaps there will always be yellow buses
passing and Presto's
and people with faces like broken promises

and shops full of stotties and butties and buckets and bubble bath
and bones for broth
where the poor may inherit the earth

and women who will
wade into the wind and waste with hope eternal
and kids like saplings planted by the Council

and William Armstrong's endless line
of bairns, whose names, in sandstone,
rehabilitate their streets of rag and bone

where bits of paper, bottle tops and Pepsi cans blow up and down
despondently, like souls on their own.
Perhaps there will always be unremembered men

and maps of Old Dunston and Metroland and the rough blown rain
and the riding down of the sun
towards Blaydon.

Gillian Allnutt

Presents from My Aunts in Pakistan

They sent me a salwar kameez
        peacock-blue,
             and another
   glistening like an orange split open,
embossed slippers, gold and black
        points curling.
   Candy-striped glass bangles
        snapped, drew blood.
   Like at school, fashions changed
       in Pakistan –
the salwar bottoms were broad and stiff,
       then narrow.
My aunts chose an apple-green sari,
   silver bordered
       for my teens.

I tried each satin-silken top –
     was alien in the sitting room.
I could never be as lovely
       as those clothes –
   I longed
for denim and corduroy.
    My costume clung to me
      and I was aflame,
I couldn't rise up out of its fire,
   half-English,
      unlike Aunt Jamila.

I wanted my parents' camel-skin lamp –
    switching it on in my bedroom,
to consider the cruelty
      and the transformation

from camel to shade,
    marvel at the colours
        like stained glass.

My mother cherished her jewellery –
    Indian gold, dangling, filigree,
        But it was stolen from our car.
The presents were radiant in my wardrobe.
    My aunts requested cardigans
        from Marks and Spencers.

My salwar kameez
    didn't impress the schoolfriend
who sat on my bed, asked to see
    my weekend clothes.
But often I admired the mirror-work,
    tried to glimpse myself
        in the miniature
glass circles, recall the story
    how the three of us
        sailed to England.
Prickly heat had me screaming on the way.
    I ended up in a cot
In my English grandmother's dining room,
    found myself alone,
        playing with a tin boat.

I pictured my birthplace
    from fifties' photographs.
        When I was older
there was conflict, a fractured land
    throbbing through newsprint.
Sometimes I saw Lahore –
        my aunts in shaded rooms,

screened from male visitors,
  sorting presents,
    wrapping them in tissue.

Or there were beggars, sweeper-girls
  and I was there –
    of no fixed nationality,
staring through fretwork
    at the Shalimar Gardens.

Moniza Alvi

Video Tale of a Patriot

for David Maxwell

START. Eton. Hice. Beaten
     in some grim urban/hopeless northern
seat. Afforded southern chances.
     Rosette. Recount. Speech. Dances.
Member. Lobbies. Froth. Committees.
     Old wife. New wife. Boards. City's.
Sir. Riches. Burgundy. Soak.
     Lord. Bypass. Bypass. Croak.

Sorry, REWIND: bypass-bypass-
     lord-soak-burgundy-riches-
sir. PLAY. 'Sir: I am increasingly
     concerned at the let's say increasingly
unpredictable, unclassifiable,
     unconstructive, unreliable,
incomprehensible, reprehensible,
     a-moral, im-moral, not very sensible

acts of citizens of England of late.
     Acts not actually threatening the State
but thoroughly disconcerting. Sir:
     I saw a her who was kissing a her.
I heard the young call enemies brothers.
     I felt my money being spent on others
lying in slums, doing nothing for it.
     I smelt filth. Though I try to ignore it

it won't go away. I see vague vicars
        plastering cars with political stickers.
I read about princes visiting thieves,
        and a lord who cares what a lout believes.
I took down the numbers of those I saw
        shouting *We don't want this no more*
outside the school where a shocking per cent
        appeared to have no idea what I meant,

or even what it means to be born
        a Briton. I tell you, a day will dawn
when everyone does what the blazes he wants,
        bangs his drums and performs his sundance
on what was once a proud green land,
        ruled with a disciplining spotless hand
correctly. Sir, a gent, I am sure, would
        agree with me when I—' STOP. FAST FORWARD.

Glyn Maxwell

Cambridge

I think it's time it withered, let us go:
the teashops, pubs, the upright girls on bikes;
the bright young men in shadowed doorways
calling clever names in code;

this softened, cheesy, gracious place
that quaintly leans to love the lounging river,
breathe its vegetable scent;
that wraps itself in tender light.,,

It's time to say enough: it's stale,
it's done to death. Let Safeways come,
McDonald's, let concrete pour,
here where the thousand bluebells lie

and dream only of bluebells, being blue.

Kate Clanchy

English Weather

January's grey and slushy,
February's chill and drear,
March is wild and wet and windy,
April seldom brings much cheer.
In May a day or two of sunshine,
Three or four in June, perhaps.
July is usually filthy,
August skies are open taps.
In September things start dying,
Then comes cold October mist.
November we make plans to spend
The best part of December pissed.

Wendy Cope

Broadmead Brook

O you haunting ghosts, I move towards you.
Could I go over these flooded plains
It would not be to any Paradise:
I came from none and I expect to find none;
It was a long journey, or so it seemed.
The scene changed, and thoughts went through my head,
But even the possibility of knowledge
– Never coveted – seemed no more than a slide
From one thing to another. First the child
Tasting the world, and finding that it hurt;
Then the youth, felled by the bolt of love,
Then labouring where the knowledge was acquired
In self-defence or else in mere ambition.
But late in time and after all deceits,
I came to stand beside Broadmead Brook
As in the very hollow of my hand.
A woman stood there who had been a child
Where in another century my mother
Had played and laboured. Now all was changed,
Yet Broadmead Brook flowed, exquisite woods
Marked her course, for in my fantasy
It was she guarded the bounding deer,
The rabbits and the partridges, and all
Who dare to dream, and be, of England still.

C.H. Sisson

AND BE MERRY

'Oh England, I'm left to summon your golden days.
A brillig of bonbon and sherbet awnings for butcher,
baker, Lipton's; the lanes wafting Yorkshire puds
with gravy that called home Brownies and Cubs.'

– Daljit Nagra

1960s

The Whitsun Weddings

That Whitsun, I was late getting away:
    Not till about
One-twenty on the sunlit Saturday
Did my three-quarters-empty train pull out,
All windows down, all cushions hot, all sense
Of being in a hurry gone. We ran
Behind the backs of houses, crossed a street
Of blinding windscreens, smelt the fish-dock; thence
The river's level drifting breadth began,
Where sky and Lincolnshire and water meet.

All afternoon, through the tall heat that slept
    For miles inland,
A slow and stopping curve southwards we kept.
Wide farms went by, short-shadowed cattle, and
Canals with floatings of industrial froth;
A hothouse flashed uniquely: hedges dipped
And rose: and now and then a smell of grass
Displaced the reek of buttoned carriage-cloth
Until the next town, new and nondescript,
Approached with acres of dismantled cars.

At first, I didn't notice what a noise
    The weddings made
Each station that we stopped at: sun destroys
The interest of what's happening in the shade,
And down the long cool platforms whoops and skirls
I took for porters larking with the mails,

And went on reading. Once we started, though,
We passed them, grinning and pomaded, girls
In parodies of fashion, heels and veils,
All posed irresolutely, watching us go,

As if out on the end of an event
        Waving goodbye
To something that survived it. Struck, I leant
More promptly out next time, more curiously,
And saw it all again in different terms:
The fathers with broad belts under their suits
And seamy foreheads; mothers loud and fat;
An uncle shouting smut; and then the perms,
The nylon gloves and jewellery-substitutes,
The lemons, mauves, and olive-ochres that

Marked off the girls unreally from the rest.
        Yes, from cafés
And banquet-halls up yards, and bunting-dressed
Coach-party annexes, the wedding-days
Were coming to an end. All down the line
Fresh couples climbed aboard: the rest stood round;
The last confetti and advice were thrown,
And, as we moved, each face seemed to define
Just what it saw departing: children frowned
At something dull; fathers had never known

Success so huge and wholly farcical;
        The women shared
The secret like a happy funeral;
While girls, gripping their handbags tighter, stared
At a religious wounding. Free at last,
And loaded with the sum of all they saw,
We hurried towards London, shuffling gouts of steam.

Now fields were building-plots, and poplars cast
Long shadows over major roads, and for
Some fifty minutes, that in time would seem

Just long enough to settle hats and say
    I nearly died,
A dozen marriages got under way.
They watched the landscape, sitting side by side
– An Odeon went past, a cooling tower,
And someone running up to bowl – and none
Thought of the others they would never meet
Or how their lives would all contain this hour.
I thought of London spread out in the sun,
Its postal districts packed like squares of wheat:

There we were aimed. And as we raced across
    Bright knots of rail
Past standing Pullmans, walls of blackened moss
Came close, and it was nearly done, this frail
Travelling coincidence; and what it held
Stood ready to be loosed with all the power
That being changed can give. We slowed again,
And as the tightened brakes took hold, there swelled
A sense of falling, like an arrow-shower
Sent out of sight, somewhere becoming rain.

Philip Larkin

1980s

The 4.15

The 4.15 from Charing Cross, juddering
its way through Sussex, spilled my carrier-bag.
A horn of plenty on the rack, it poured
a half-erect telescopic umbrella,
some black seamed tights and jasmine tea, wet gloves,
a slow cascade of books (mercifully
the Tampax stayed aloft). The final touch −
a box from the Loon Moon Supermarket
(sweetened kumquats) hit an old military type
in the balls. He took it well.

The four men opposite were all smiling
after my ritual of apologies.
They'd read the *Love Life* lying on the floor
as something other than a Poetry book.

Fiona Pitt-Kethley

Lonely Hearts

Can someone make my simple wish come true?
Male biker seeks female for touring fun.
Do you live in North London? Is it you?

Gay vegetarian whose friends are few,
I'm into music, Shakespeare and the sun.
Can someone make my simple wish come true?

Executive in search of something new –
Perhaps bisexual woman, arty young,
Do you live in North London? Is it you?

Successful, straight and solvent? I am too –
Attractive Jewish lady with a son.
Can someone make my simple wish come true?

I'm Libran, inexperienced and blue –
Need slim non-smoker under twenty-one.
Do you live in North London? Is it you?

Please write (with photo) to Box 152.
Who knows where it may lead once we've begun.
Can someone make my simple wish come true?
Do you live in North London? Is it you?

Wendy Cope

England at Christmas, 1982

O silly little, proud and silly, country
so good at ceremonial, limited wars,
football (occasionally)! Snob Billy Buntery
gives all the rich, rich presents – Santa Claus
has handed out the land. He hates the serfs,
the common people, so uncommonly low;
loves dogs, cats, hunting, cricket, the green turfs
that make a stately-homely postcard show –
quite beautiful, memorials to old greed,
when what there was to take, to steal, to pinch
went to the bastard Baron on his steed
or landowners, enclosing each square inch,

or City men, who raise a joyous anthem
for a fake-lady bossyboots from Grantham.

Gavin Ewart

Sister of the Planets

Remembering Imogen Holst

I saw her glide, lighter than air
Across the lawn, musical
And quick as the dancer she'd have been
Had music not possessed her;
Then on the Mere, her shallop a punt
From which, with singing gesture,
She ruled the Elements – conducted
Madrigals, Byrd, Morley, Gibbons...
Britten, Pears and twenty more
On moored punts picked their way
Through polyphonic dreams –
'Though Amaryllis dance in green';
'April is in my mistress' face';
'Adieu sweet Amaryllis'.

Content with Planet Earth,
This child of Holst who fathered also
The Planets – all, that is,
Except this Earth. Able
To fly on her own wings of song
She cherished Terra Firma,
The great Tudor voices, a taste
Of warm Burgundian song (and wine),
Her father's voice, Ben Britten's
In his last flight, and this
Acre of Suffolk where,
Having written the last word
On what meant most to her,
She laid down her pen, lay down
To sleep, and slipped away.

Edward Lowbury

Costa Brava

A cooling tide slakes the vanilla shore;
the supine English roast their cares away
burnishing peeling shoulders to the roar
of Boney M or Rock on Saturday
—los duros por el jukebox, por favor.

Doreen and Reggie order drinks, unsure
of what precisely fluent natives say;
phrasebooks are useless, scattered on the floor
of Manuel's bar, and Tonio's café.
¿Cervezas grandes? Gracias, señor.

Doreen likes food that Reggie finds a bore
—helados, pollos, calamars, tal vez—
preferring naked mermaids to implore
his hunger on the topless beach today.
Dame melocotones, por favor.

Gracias. De nada. Would you like some more?
No hablo español, dispensame.
¿Cuanto es esta? How much? Are you sure?
Dos mil pesetas, Doreen, that's okay.
¿Y el retrete? ¿Donde es, señor?

A fortnight in the sun. What's language for
but dressing up in to go out and play?
Doreen and Reggie, Lancashire before,
return as *La Dorita* and *El Rey.*
¿Turistas? Más amigos, por favor.
¿Que bella Costa Brava es, señor!

John Gohorry

Apple Gatherers

Stanley Spencer, 1913

Each night, for the men,
a dole of stoat's-piss cider in the barn.
Women had homes to go to.

Dossing in straw
his head was filled with apples, apples. He saw
Martha, plain dull Martha,

in a smudged green sunlight
coming steady as a queen to her confinement,
apron bellied full

of fruit. Then Boy Jack
goosed her, hooting as her hands went up
and all the apples spilled

out from her, sound-
lessly, endlessly, helplessly down.
They'd bruise and spoil.

At dawn the slow ache
of the job resumed. Tree by tree, back to back
they worked closer, within reach.

Neither turned or spoke
as he slipped her the prize of his pick.
Their forearms touched.

What passed between them?
In a freak of sunlight they saw generations
    like as apples, spilling

    from them, heat-
tranced puppets, bobbing, aching in a sweet
    druggy smell of fermentation.

    She saw a frump of a girl
who coveted one beauty for herself
    and bit. She saw the slug

    in its flesh-pit, glutting
in all innocence. He saw the rootling
    snout of the old pink sow,

    shrill piglets squabbling
into her as she rolled – her flabby grin,
    her battery of dugs – and

    Master's coming, quick!
he saw a boy thrash the pigs off with a stick.
    The apple dropped and lay.

    The picture's dated
1913. Next year she'd be picking again
    alongside raw boys and old men.

Philip Gross

Midsummer (XXXVI)

The oak inns creak in their joints as light declines
from the ale-coloured skies of Warwickshire.
Autumn has blown the froth from the foaming orchards,
so white-haired regulars draw chairs nearer the grate
to spit on logs that crackle into leaves of fire.
But they grow deafer, not sure if what they hear
is the drone of the abbeys from matins to compline,
or the hornet's nest of a chain saw working late
on the knoll up there back of the Norman chapel.
Evening loosens the moth, the owl shifts its weight,
a fish-mouthed moon swims up from wavering elms,
but four old men are out on the garden benches,
talking of the bows they have drawn, their strings of wenches,
their coined eyes shrewdly glittering like the Thames'
estuaries. I heard their old talk carried
through cables laid across the Atlantic bed,
their gossip rustles like an apple orchard's
in my own head, and I can drop their names
like familiars – those bastard grandsires
whose maker granted them a primal pardon –
because the worm that cores the rotting apple
of the world and the hornet's chain saw cannot touch the words
of Shallow or Silence in their fading garden.

Derek Walcott

Summer in the Country

'Strawberries', 'raspberries', whisper the letters
Until July is a taste, to hide
In reddened mouths, in fields which feet
Can't flatten, tall, soft throbbed with heat.
Where horses shaking gnats aside
Come slow to hand through the darkening grass

Where seeds fall too, from willow trees
(Rooted in damp, an ancient drain)
White silk clings to my back. I see
Small clouds pass slowly overhead.
Ask me nothing. In harvest fields
Drivers wear masks – cough dust; hear grain
Hiss profit; loss. But in the shade
Pale seed drops lightly over me.

The harvest ends. White webs of cold
Are strung across the sun;
The wind blows now no hint of fruit
but draught, unease, what's done; undone.

Alison Brackenbury

Summer Pudding

for Carole Reeves

Begin with half a pound of raspberries
picked from the deep end of your sloping garden, where the birds
  lay hopscotch in the draggled fruitnets; add
a quarter of redcurrants; gently seethe in orange juice
  for six or seven minutes with some sugar,
giving the pan a ritual shake from time to time, inducing
  a marriage of those fine, compatible
tastes; and leave to cool. An open kitchen door invites
  whatever breeze will help itself to flavour,
attenuating it downhill across your neighbours' gardens
  (be generous!) so summer will surprise them,
an unidentifiable recalled fulfilment haunting
  the giant bellflower and the scarlet runners.
Now introduce your strawberries, sliced to let the pallid heartsflesh
  transfuse its juice into the mass, transmute
cooled fruit to liquid crystal while you line your bowl with bread
  and add the mixture – keeping back some juice –
lid it with bread, cover and weight it, chill it if you like
  (as if the winter took a hand) and hoard it,
opus magnum ripening its secret, edible,
  inviolable time. And when you dare
slide your knife round its socket to uncling – a sudden suck –
  this gelid Silbury mined with the wealth
of archetypal summer, let it be on one of three
  occasions: for a kitchenful of children
whose mouths grow purpleringed and flecked with whipped
    cream as they dig
  and lose, entranced, the treasure of the minute;

or for the friends around your polished table, when that soft
    lake of mahogany reflects the faces
melting in candlelight and burgundy, rivers of talk
    eddying to a stillness lost in taste
primitive as a language, clear as thought; or for whoever
    will join you in your garden when the sun
carries out summer to the edge of dark, and stay to eat
    there in the early chill as twilight gels
and owlhoots quiver from the gulf of darkness, where a floodlit
    cathedral floats under your eyes, and still
(wreckage of smeared plates and clotted spoons piling the table)
    after the lights are killed and the cathedral
vanishes like a switchedoff hologram, remain to plot
    the moon's progress across the brimming air
scaled by the nightscented stocks, or with binoculars
    arrest the Brownian movement of the stars.

Grevel Lindop

As the West End Allegro Subsides Today

for Landeg White, 1975

When you went on about those Trinidadian
Steel Bands and calypso in your Chichiri flat
I did not really care; I nodded only out of
Goodwill nor did I expect the winds to blow
Us into another flat on Chepstow Road
And one London summer afternoon watch
The whole carnival, colourful, brisk, gently
Flowing towards Notting Hill Gate
Graced by tuneful steel bands as baby
Martin watching cricket on TV pulled out
The plugs fidgeting about being left alone
To learn to crawl. But as the West End
Allegro subsides today and the periodic
Blurt of Zomba muezzins carelessly mingles
With the croaking crows of Chirunga
Estate to consummate our re-entry into
An otherwise cautious quiet green, tempers
Often fray – shouldn't I have cared at all?

Jack Mapanje

Wailing in Wandsworth

Lovers who would pet and fondle
All along the River Wandle,
Running down through Wandsworth Town
      Leafily, are gone.
Factory excreta tumble,
Gangs prowl, sniffing out a rumble,
      And the cops move on
Cottagers disposed to fumble
In their lowly dwelling, humble
      Public jakes or john.

Where the lovers used to ramble
Adult Aid chain owners amble,
Strolling down through Wandsworth Town,
      Counting up the cash.
By the bridge, his fourteenth tipple
Claims the drunk, who takes a triple
      Length-and-value slash,
And the alders wind would ripple,
Poplar, beech rain loved to stipple,
      Are not even ash.

Still and all, I shouldn't grumble,
I who sit alone and mumble,
Writing down in Wandsworth Town
      My troubled Double Dutch.
I would never cause to stumble
From its grave, but let it crumble,
      Ancient pain, as such.

By the waters of the Wandle
Where the lovers used to fondle,
Where I craft this rhubarb rondel,
Life is better: much.

Kit Wright

A Prayer to Live with Real People

Let me not live, ever, without fat people,
the marshmallow flesh set thick on the muscular bone,
the silk white perms of sweet sixteen-stone ladies,
luscious as pom-poms or full blown perfumed magnolias,
breasts like cottage loaves dropped into lace-knit sweaters,
all cream-bun arms and bottoms in sticky leathers.
O Russian dolls, O range of hills
rosy behind the glo-green park of the pool table,
thorns are not neater or sharper than your delicate shoes.

Let me not live, ever, without pub people,
the tattooed forearm steering the cue like a pencil,
the twelve-pint belly who adds up the scores in his head,
the wiry owner of whippets, the keeper of ferrets,
thin wives who suffer, who are silent, who talk with their eyes,
the girl who's discovered that sex is for she who tries.
O zebra blouse, O vampish back
blown like a lily from the swaying stalk of your skirt,
roses are not more ruthless than your silver-pink lipstick.

And let me live, always and forever among neighbours like these
who order their year by the dates of the leek competitions,
who care sacrificially for Jack Russell terriers and pigeons,
who read very carefully captions in *The Advertiser* and *Echo*
which record their successes and successes of teams they support,
whose daughters grow up and marry friends' boys from Crook.
O wedding gifts, O porcelain flowers
twined on their vases under the lace-lipped curtains
save me from Habitat, and snobbery and too damn much literary ambition.

Anne Stevenson

RECESSIONAL

'All this
A cipher for what England is – or was.'
– *Stuart Henson*

1970s

Three Knights

from 'In England' (1976)

In the old abbey chancel, in the apse, on the floor,
three knights sleep their last sleep, gleaming
in the chancel's gloom like stone sturgeon,
scales of chain-mail, armor-plate gills. All three
hawk-nosed and hatchet-faced, head-to-heel
knights: in breastplate, helmet, long sword. And sleep
longer than they woke. Dusk in the chancel. Arms
crossed on the chest, like carps.

The flash follows the camera's click – a kind
of shot (anything that hurls us forward
on to the wall of the future's a shot). The three,
frozen still, enact once again within
the camera what has already taken place – at Poitiers,
or the Holy Land: a traveler in a straw hat is,
for those who died for Father, Son,
and Holy Ghost, more fearful than the Saracen.

The abbey sprawled at ease along the riverbank.
Clumps of green trees. White butterflies
flutter over flower beds by the chapter house.
The cool of an English noonday. In England, as nowhere else,
nature, rather than diverting, soothes the eye;
and under the chancel wall, as if before
a theater curtain lowered once and for all,
the hawthorn's applause singles out none of them with its call.

Joseph Brodsky, *translated by Alan Myers*

The Vanished Places

At Dunwich, you feel like a trespasser on the earth:
    on sunken paths through the mushroom-scented wood,
past the last monastery wall and the last gravestone
    (John Brinkley Easey, uneasy at the brink)
to the cliffs' edge and the last church tower out at sea.
    They say the bells still peal, perhaps to restore
some tenuous hope of immortality, while bones
    gesture a final desultory farewell.

Trespasser? Tenant? Neither will win, the sea insists,
    in the vanished places – Dunwich, Walberswick –
where lanes scrawl to the margin of a torn-off coastline
    whose history is rewritten by the tide.
Think, the sea persists, of your monuments and cities,
    skills and crafts, in the scale of natural time;
and then remember eleven Dunwich churches drowned
    off this temporary coast; tread carefully.

Too simple to wish a lingering death concluded:
    'the halo of traditionary splendour'
(the Reverend Alfred Suckling, 1848)
    still glimmers here in the wasted vacancy.
A scything north-easterly wind, sleet across the sea,
    and a burdened sky weigh down upon the land:
trespasser, tenant, walk tentatively here,
    your world undercut by erosive waters.

Neil Powell

Mercian Hymns (I)

King of the perennial holly-groves, the riven sand-
    stone: overlord of the M5: architect of the his-
    toric rampart and ditch, the citadel at Tamworth,
    the summer hermitage in Holy Cross: guardian of
    the Welsh Bridge and the Iron Bridge: contractor
    to the desirable new estates: saltmaster: money-
    changer: commissioner for oaths: martyrologist:
    the friend of Charlemagne.

'I liked that,' said Offa, 'sing it again.'

Geoffrey Hill

Time Removed

I go on and on in England
and walk no ground untrodden.

Landscapes are checkered –
tamed out of new years
and recurring generations.

Compulsive hands have shaped
bordered fields
out of scrub,
rivers' faces with bridge,
edifices for trees towering
lands now railed and tarred.

Animals are not bony and bare.
Wheels quicken time –
through a late summer
staying fresh as spring.

And here
just as jungles hold my love
every whiff of air evokes a time
like the horse my father left
and I after ten years away
found the greyhaired skeleton
neighing to me,
like these days do,
in memories too overlaid to touch.

James Berry

Ploughland

They drudged across the season's palimpsest,
The feathered horses, driven into rain;
Their dapples and attendant shades impressed
Upon the skies which pulled them up the lane.
   Light moves about the knotted ploughland, sown
   With undistinguished seeds of chalk and bone.

A sullen field, pegged out with brittle trees,
A watercolour of the English School;
Her pawky hedgerows crumble to their knees,
The locked fires in her fractured flint lie cool.
   Old weathers broke her in, and we retrace
   The crows' feet etched on her dissolving face.

The lost teams and their leaders. All that care
Is mere commemoration by the wind.
A shower of bells freckles the cooling air;
Our booted feet drag with an awkward rind.
   Down in the levelled churchyard a few graves
   Remind the birds how well the past behaves,

Working along the bent flow of the land
With no more substance than our thought makes good:
A face limned on the air, a tenuous hand
To scribble in the margins of the wood.
   A rash of brickwork rubricates their claim:
   A foundered house, and a forgotten name.

The Home Farm lacked a tenant forty years,
Pigs littered grandly in the living room;
The rain is flighted with her children's tears,
A burnt tree's crater beckons to the tomb.

One old man with his dog slows up the hill;
A shooting party spaces out the chill

Where scatterings of green remind the day
Of beasts long cropped and felled: the molten dead
Still driving purpose through the common clay
In new returns of sacramental bread.
                    The harnessed bells ride out upon their round,
                    Tossing cold heads above the burdened ground.

Peter Scupham

The Branch Line

One train was the last.
Decorated with a crowd
Of people who like last things,
Not normally travellers,
Mostly children and their fathers,
It left to a theatrical blast
As the guard for once played
At his job, with mixed feelings.

Photographers were there,
For the only time perhaps
Since the railway groped
Down into these shires
First of all, and the squires
Fretted about their deer.
There were flags and a few maps,
And cheers as the signal dropped.

The platform is now old
And empty, but still shows
The act of waiting.
Beyond it the meadows
Where once the toy shadows
Of funnel and smoke bowled,
Are pure green, and no echoes
Squeeze into the cutting.

The villages that gave
The stations their names
Were always out of sight,
Behind a hill, up a lane,

Dead, except when a train
Fetched somebody forth alive
But now no one at all comes
Out of them by this route.

If the particular fast
Bright dragon of childhood
Is null, I feel the same,
Extinct; not obsolete
Nor dead, but lightweight.
The line has left no ghost
Even, but is as void
As my discarded name.

My past has been defaced
Because it ran together
So often with this line.
Trains exist elsewhere
But different, sinister:
Heads, looking out for a last
Goodbye, freeze and weather
To the sky, as at Tyburn.

Patricia Beer

Strike

The earth comes moist-looking, and blackens;
a trickle of earth where the feet pressed,
twice a day, wearing off the grass.
Where the miners
were seen: a letter blown damply
into the corner of a hut: 'Oh dear love, come to me'
and nothing else.

Where are they?
The sheep bleat back to the mist balding
with terror; where
are they? The miners
are under the ground.

A pale blue patch of thick worsted
a scrag of cotton;
the wheel is still that washed the pounded ore.
They were cut down.

Almost turned by water, a stammer of the huge wheel
groping at the bearings.
Their bayonets; the red coat
gluey with red.

The water shrinks
to its source. The wheel,
in balance.

Jon Silkin

Gladstone Street

It was the place to go in nineteen-thirty,
And so we went. A housemaid or two
Still lingered on at the bigger houses.
A miner and his family were the next
To follow us there, had scarcely settled in
When the wife began dying, whitely visible
Through the bay window in their double bed.
At the back, the garden vanished
Under grass and a ramshackle shed.
People were sure the street was going downhill.
It literally was: cracks in our hall
Opened as the house started to subside
Towards the mines beneath. Miners were everywhere
Under that cancerous hill. My mother swore
That you could hear them tapping away below
Of a quiet night. Miners unnerved her so
Ever since one sat beside her on the train
And soiled her with his pit dirt. But it wasn't miners
Undid the street. The housemaids lasted
Until the war, then fed the factories.
Flat-dwellers came and went, in the divided houses,
Mothers unwedded who couldn't pay their rent.
A race of gardeners died, and a generation
Hacked down the walls to park their cars
Where the flowers once were. It was there it showed,
The feeble-minded style of the neighbourhood
Gone gaudily mad in painted corrugations,
Botches of sad carpentry. The street front has scarcely changed.
No one has recorded the place.
Perhaps we shall become sociology. We have outpaced
Gladstone's century. We might have been novels.

Charles Tomlinson

Reformation

The hazed meadows of England grow over chancels
Where cattle hooves kick up heraldic tiles
And molehills heap their spoils above slumped walls.
The cruck-beamed roofs of refectories nestle under
Sheds and barns, hay piled high where
Augustine and Aquinas chapter by chapter
Were read in these now lapsed pastoral acres.

Small streams wash the smashed crockery of Cistercians.
Stone-plaited carvings are wedged in gable ends
Of farmhouses, springs irrigate robbed chapels
Where all is marsh, reeds meshed among cracked altars.
A buzzard shrieks *yaa-i* in a tall tree.
Plainchant echoing along the valleys.
High hedges stand above spoiled finials.

And Sunday mornings see small meeting houses,
Reformed parishes and tabernacles,
Bethesdas and the whole wide countryside,
All split seven ways in sect and congregation,
Assembling to praise God from whom all blessings
Flow through his derelict priories, abbeys, cells
The afternoon sun will show, faint shadows among fields.

Anthony Thwaite

Returning from Church

That country spire – Samuel Palmer knew
What world they entered, who,
Kneeling in English village pew
Were near those angels whose golden effigies looked down
From Gothic vault or hammer-beam.
Grave sweet ancestral faces
Beheld, Sunday by Sunday, a holy place
Few find who, pausing now
In empty churches, cannot guess
At those deep simple states of grace.

Kathleen Raine

At the Castle Hotel, Taunton

Today it's not scones but tea-cakes
    (And the sound of ambulances
    in the reconstructed streets) –

Rich voices are discussing the new Warden
    (The Show is the best for years,
    the architects' watercolours outstanding) –

Pearls and brogues survive, cashmere clings
    (Is this the Ark of Adultery
    or two old friends killing time?) –

Interlopers must wait for their tea
    (There's only one waitress on today,
    her footsteps are masked on the stairs) –

Hands want something to do, eyes won't idle
    (*Country Life* in a rexine folder:
    who buys, who sells all these houses?) –

O impossible England under the modern stars
    (Mr Edward du Cann thanks the voters
    of Taunton for their generous support) –

So much beauty, so unexpectedly preserved
    (And we two strangers have today
    honoured gentle Eliot at East Coker) –

Not only the pheasant eating by the road
    (And the cider factory, the industrial
    archaeology with the rural) –

But the pattern of beauty changing in the air
    (Fields painted by history, a steam
    of seasons softening what lives) –

Somerset for survivors and a good thing too
    (Seventeenth-century farmhouse,
    part-converted, owner abroad) –

Seen from Ilminster spire, everything is safe
    (It is being kept for posterity
    but where do the people of England live?)

Peter Porter

By Rail through the Earthly Paradise, Perhaps Bedfordshire

The fishermen among the fireweed.

Towpath and humpbacked bridge. Cows
in one field, slabs of hay
ranged in another.

Common day
precious to me.
There's nothing else
to grasp.

The train
moves me past it too fast, not much,
just a little, I don't want
to stay for ever.
                    Horses,
three of them, flowing across a paddock
as wind flows over barley.

Oaks in parkland, distinct,
growing their shadows.
A man from Cairo across from me
reading *A Synopsis of Eye Physiology*.
The brickworks,
fantastical slender chimneys.

I'm not hungry,
not lonely. It seems
at times I want nothing,

no human giving and taking.
Nothing I see
fails to give pleasure,

no thirst for righteousness
dries my throat, I am silent
and happy, and troubled only
by my own happiness. Looking,

looking and naming. I wish the train now
would halt for me at a station in the fields,
(the name goes by
unread).
     In the deep aftermath
of its faded rhythm, I could become

a carved stone
set in the gates of the earthly paradise,

an angler's fly
lost in the sedge to watch the centuries.

Denise Levertov

Leavings

A soft whoosh, the sunset blaze
of straw on blackened stubble,
a thatch-deep, freshening
barbarous crimson burn –

I rode down England
as they fired the crop
that was the leavings of a crop,
the smashed tow-coloured barley,

down from Ely's Lady Chapel,
the sweet tenor Latin
forever banished,
the sumptuous windows

threshed clear by Thomas Cromwell.
Which circle does he tread,
scalding on cobbles,
each one a broken statue's head?

After midnight, after summer,
to walk in a sparking field,
to smell dew and ashes
and start Will Brangwen's ghost

from the hot soot –
a breaking sheaf of light,
abroad in the hiss
and clash of stooking.

Seamus Heaney

Sad Grave of an Imperial Mongoose

Under this weeping ash or umbrella tree
protrudes among white and purple crocuses
the small tombstone of a mongoose
inscribed 'Darling Riki-tiki. R.I.P.'

He died because, when brought 'home'
by a senior member of the Indian Civil Service
on his retirement he could not stand of course the cold
climate of this green vale. And now the Raj having gone,

the Civil Servant having gone (at one of the two universities
of the time he began with a first class degree in the
classical learning, largely, of a former empire), his children too
having gone (he – and they – were cremated and scattered, but he has

an entry in *Who Was Who*), the house as well having changed hands
into other families, this stone among broken crocuses over the small
ribs of Riki-tiki pierced a few inches down by threads from
crocus corms and wandering rootlets of the umbrella tree

remains – other than the entry in *Who Was Who* and a short piece
imprisoned flatly in a huge back volume of *The Times* – the sole
indication of the career of one who said
'Many of my best friends are Indians', also 'Habeas Corpus hardly

could apply to Indians'; as he administered justice
Socratic and Ciceronian under the aegis – a phrase
whose broad propriety he would have
understood – of after all,

an uninspiriting empire. Though it is easy to look back.

Geoffrey Grigson

[172]

The Shoot

They are bringing the bright birds down.
The winter trees are shaken, the sky looks on
   And, far away, a town
Writes its houses on a sky with no sun.
   They are bringing the bright birds down.

   And from my room I can see
Patches of snow which the thaw hasn't reached yet,
   And now I seem to be
Alone. The wind goes off. What birds wait,
   Birds I cannot see?

   And then anger comes on fast.
I storm inwardly at these cold men
   Who will be glad to have passed
An afternoon giving the bright birds pain
   And a violent death at last.

   They are bringing the bright birds down.
Yesterday's pheasant will plummet through the air.
   And I am not guiltless, I own,
For I have eaten pheasants who shelter here.
   I too have brought them down.

Elizabeth Jennings

Last Load

Baled hay out in a field
Five miles from home. Barometer falling.
A muffler of still cloud padding the stillness.
The day after day of blue scorch up to yesterday,
The heavens of dazzling iron, that seemed unalterable,
Hard now to remember.

Now, tractor bounding along lanes, among echoes,
The trailer bouncing, all its iron shouting
Under sag-heavy leaves
That seem ready to drip with stillness.
Cheek in the air alert for the first speck.

You feel sure the rain's already started –
But for the tractor's din you'd hear it hushing
In all the leaves. But still not one drop
On your face or arm. You can't believe it.
Then hoicking bales, as if at a contest. Leaping
On and off the tractor as at a rodeo.

Hurling the bales higher. The loader on top
Dodging like a monkey. The fifth layer full
Then a teetering sixth. Then for a seventh
A row down the middle. And if a bale topples
You feel you've lost those seconds forever.
Then roping it all tight, like a hard loaf.

Then fast as you dare, watching the sky
And watching the load, and feeling the air darken
With wet electricity,
The load foaming through leaves, and wallowing
Like a tug-boat meeting the open sea –

The tractor's front wheels rearing up, as you race,
And pawing the air. Then all hands
Pitching the bales off, in under a roof,
Anyhow, then back for the last load.

And now as you dash through the green light
You see between dark trees
On all the little emerald hills
The desperate loading, under the blue cloud.

Your sweat tracks through your dust, your shirt flaps chill,
And bales multiply out of each other
All down the shorn field ahead.
The faster you fling them up, the more there are of them –
Till suddenly the field's grey empty. It's finished.

And a tobacco reek breaks in your nostrils
As the rain begins
Softly and vertically silver, the whole sky softly
Falling into the stubble all round you

The trees shake out their masses, joyful,
Drinking the downpour.
The hills pearled, the whole distance drinking
And the earth-smell warm and thick as smoke

And you go, and over the whole land
Like singing heard across evening water
The tall loads are swaying towards their barns
Down the deep lanes.

Ted Hughes

REBELLION

'You've been Englished but you won't forget it, never.'
— Anne Rouse

1980s

Rules for Beginners

They said: 'Honour thy father and thy mother.
Don't spend every evening at the Disco.
Listen to your teachers, take an O level
or two. Of course, one day you'll have children.
We've tried our best to make everything nice.
Now it's up to you to be an adult!'

She went to all the 'X' films like an adult.
Sometimes she hung around the Mecca Disco.
Most of the boys she met were dead O level,
smoking and swearing, really great big children.
She had a lot of hassle with her mother;
it was always her clothes or her friends that weren't nice.

At school some of the teachers were quite nice,
but most of them thought they were minding children.
'Now Susan,' they would say, 'You're nearly adult –
behave like one!' The snobs taking O level
never had fun, never went to the Disco;
they did their homework during *Listen with Mother.*

She said: 'I'd hate to end up like my mother,
but there's this lovely bloke down at the Disco
who makes me feel a lot more like an adult.'
He murmured – 'When I look at you, it's nice
all over! Can't you cut that old O level
scene? Christ, I could give you twenty children!'

He had to marry her. There were three children –
all girls. Sometimes she took them to her mother
to get a break. She tried to keep them nice.
It was dull all day with kids, the only adult.
She wished they'd told you that, instead of O level.
Sometimes she dragged her husband to the Disco.

She got a part-time job at the Disco,
behind the bar; a neighbour had the children.
Now she knew all about being an adult
and honestly it wasn't very nice.
Her husband grumbled – 'Where's the dinner, mother?'
'I'm going down the night-school for an O level,

I am,' said mother. 'Have fun at the Disco,
kids! When you're an adult, life's all O level.
Stay clear of children, keep your figures nice!'

Carol Rumens

1960s

Diary of a Rebel

For my fierce hot-blooded sulkiness
I need the cafe – where old mats
Of paper lace catch upon coatsleeves
That are brilliant with the nap of idleness

...And the cant of the meat-fly is eternal!
On the window is the milk of lazy breath,
And the coalcart rumbles – with huge purses
Full of dust and narcotics for the masses!

Sin pricks me like a convict's suit of arrows
For here my evil, blue, and moody youth
Has found its old lair... at the bottom
Of the soil path in the bed of stinging nettles

That are splashed with wood milk
And have every hair upon them raised to strike!
There is no trade can lure me out with bundle,
Noose, and feeding-bag; I know that fate

Has graves to fill in daily life,
And the jargon of the meat-fly's leaded wing
To put to sleep the citizen
Employed in keeping worms at bay by breathing.

Rosemary Tonks

Adolescence

After the history has been made,
and when Wallace's shaggy head

glares on London from a spike, when
the exiled general is again

gliding into Athens harbour
now as embittered foreigner,

when the lean creatures crawl out of
camps and in silence try to live,

I pass foundations of houses,
walking through the wet spring, my knees

drenched from high grass charged with water,
and am part, still, of the done war.

Thom Gunn

Mrs Albion You've Got a Lovely Daughter

for Allen Ginsberg

Albion's most lovely daughter sat on the banks of the
   Mersey dangling her landing stage in the water.

The daughters of Albion
   arriving by underground at Central Station
   eating hot ecclescakes at the Pierhead
   writing 'Billy Blake is fab' on a wall in Mathew St

   taking off their navyblue schooldrawers and
   putting on nylon panties ready for the night

The daughters of Albion
   see the moonlight beating down on them in Bebington
   throw away their chewinggum ready for the goodnight kiss
sleep in the dinnertime sunlight with old men
   looking up their skirts in St Johns Gardens
comb their darkblonde hair in suburban bedrooms
powder their delicate little nipples/wondering if tonight will be the night
their bodies pressed into dresses or sweaters
lavender at The Cavern or pink at The Sink

The daughters of Albion
   wondering how to explain why they didn't go home

The daughters of Albion
   taking the dawn ferry to tomorrow
   worrying about what happened
   worrying about what hasn't happened
   lacing up blue sneakers over brown ankles
   fastening up brown stockings to blue suspenderbelts

Beautiful boys with bright red guitars
in the spaces between the stars

Reelin' an' a-rockin'
Wishin' an' a-hopin'
Kissin' an' a-prayin'
Lovin' an' a-layin'

Mrs Albion you've got a lovely daughter.

Adrian Henri

Telephone Conversation

The price seemed reasonable, location
Indifferent. The landlady swore she lived
Off premises. Nothing remained
But self-confession. 'Madam,' I warned,
'I hate a wasted journey – I am African.'
Silence. Silenced transmission of
Pressurised good-breeding. Voice, when it came,
Lipstick coated, long gold-rolled
Cigarette-holder pipped. Caught I was, foully.
'HOW DARK?'... I had not misheard... 'ARE YOU LIGHT
OR VERY DARK?' Button B. Button A. Stench
Of rancid breath of public hide-and-speak.
Red booth. Red pillar-box. Red double-tiered
Omnibus squelching tar. It *was* real! Shamed
By ill-mannered silence, surrender
Pushed dumbfounded to beg simplification.
Considerate she was, varying the emphasis –
'ARE YOU DARK? OR VERY LIGHT?' Revelation came.
'You mean – like plain or milk chocolate?'
Her assent was clinical, crushing in its light
Impersonality. Rapidly, wave-length adjusted,
I chose. 'West African sepia' – and as afterthought,
'Down in my passport.' Silence for spectroscopic
Flight of fancy, till truthfulness clanged her accent
Hard on the mouthpiece. 'WHAT'S THAT?' conceding
'DON'T KNOW WHAT THAT IS.' 'Like brunette.'
'THAT'S DARK, ISN'T IT?' 'Not altogether.
Facially, I am brunette, but madam, you should see
The rest of me. Palm of my hand, soles of my feet
Are a peroxide blond. Friction, caused –
Foolishly madam – by sitting down, has turned

My bottom raven black – One moment madam!' – sensing
Her receiver rearing on the thunderclap
About my ears – 'Madam,' I pleaded, 'wouldn't you rather
See for yourself?'

Wole Soyinka

A Poem about Poems about Vietnam

The spotlights had you covered [*thunder
in the wings*]. In the combat zones
and in the Circle, darkness. Under
the muzzles of the microphones
you opened fire, and a phalanx
of loudspeakers shook on the wall;
but all your cartridges were blanks
when you were at the Albert Hall.

Lord George Byron cared for Greece,
Auden and Cornford cared for Spain,
confronted bullets and disease
to make their poems' meaning plain;
but you – by what right did you wear
suffering like a service medal,
numbing the nerve that they laid bare,
when you were at the Albert Hall?

The poets of another time –
Owen with a rifle butt
between his paper and the slime,
Donne quitting Her pillow to cut
a quill – knew that in love and war
dispatches from the front are all.
We believe them, they were there,
when you were at the Albert Hall.

Poet, they whisper in their sleep
louder from underground than all
the mikes that hung upon your lips
when you were at the Albert Hall.

Jon Stallworthy

Demo against the Vietnam War, 1968

Praise just one thing in London, he challenged,
as if everybody, everything, owned a minus,
was damnable, and the Inner Circle led to hell;
and I thought, allowed one slot only,
what, in October, would I choose?

Not the blurred grasslands of a royal, moody park
where great classy trees lurk in mist;
not the secretive Thames either, silvering
its slow knots through the East End –
sooty scenes, good for Antonioni panning soft
atmospheric shots, emblems of isolation,
prologue to the elegiac Square, the house where,
suddenly, lemon oblongs spring to windows.

Nor would I choose the stylised catalogue
of torment in the National Gallery.
Better that tatty group, under Nelson's column,
their home-made banners held aloft,
their small cries of 'Peace, Peace,' impotent;
also the moment with the tannoy turned off,
the thudding wings of pigeons audible,
the shredding fountains, once again, audible.

So praise to the end of the march,
their songs, their jargon, outside the Embassy.
Yes, this I'd choose: their ardour, their naivety,
violence of commitment, cruelty of devotion,
'We shall not be moved, We shall overcome' –
despite sullen police concealed in vans
waiting for arclights to fail, for furtive darkness,
and camera teams, dismantled, all breezing home.

Dannie Abse

Nadir

End-of-June blackbird and blue tit came
to the garden today, shabbied by fatherhood
– white sideburns streaked, black coat
unpreened and broken – silent now too
because the courting's over. I sympathised
with them, knowing that fledgling shouts left
little time for niceties of toilet.

                Yet I imagined,
although I knew it wasn't so, that I saw
in them some remnants of that horrified surprise
the movement in the nest had given them
who had no intention of creation,
shock at the squirming life where there had been
only the soothing eggs to ease the nesting itch.

Their round eyes stared, they seemed still dumbfounded.

Molly Holden

Elm

for Ruth Fainlight

I know the bottom, she says. I know it with my great tap root:
It is what you fear.
I do not fear it: I have been there.

Is it the sea you hear in me,
Its dissatisfactions?
Or the voice of nothing, that was your madness?

Love is a shadow.
How you lie and cry after it
Listen: these are its hooves: it has gone off, like a horse.

All night I shall gallop thus, impetuously,
Till your head is a stone, your pillow a little turf,
Echoing, echoing.

Or shall I bring you the sound of poisons?
This is rain now, this big hush.
And this is the fruit of it: tin-white, like arsenic.

I have suffered the atrocity of sunsets.
Scorched to the root
My red filaments burn and stand, a hand of wires.

Now I break up in pieces that fly about like clubs.
A wind of such violence
Will tolerate no bystanding: I must shriek.

The moon, also, is merciless: she would drag me
Cruelly, being barren.
Her radiance scathes me. Or perhaps I have caught her.

I let her go. I let her go
Diminished and flat, as after radical surgery.
How your bad dreams possess and endow me.

I am inhabited by a cry.
Nightly it flaps out
Looking, with its hooks, for something to love.

I am terrified by this dark thing
That sleeps in me;
All day I feel its soft, feathery turnings, its malignity.

Clouds pass and disperse.
Are those the faces of love, those pale irretrievables?
Is it for such I agitate my heart?

I am incapable of more knowledge.
What is this, this face
So murderous in its strangle of branches?——

Its snaky acids hiss.
It petrifies the will. These are the isolate, slow faults
That kill, that kill, that kill.

Sylvia Plath

Homage to a Government

Next year we are to bring the soldiers home
For lack of money, and it is all right.
Places they guarded, or kept orderly,
Must guard themselves, and keep themselves orderly.
We want the money for ourselves at home
Instead of working. And this is all right.

It's hard to say who wanted it to happen,
But now it's been decided nobody minds.
The places are a long way off, not here,
Which is all right, and from what we hear
The soldiers there only made trouble happen.
Next year we shall be easier in our minds.

Next year we shall be living in a country
That brought its soldiers home for lack of money.
The statues will be standing in the same
Tree-muffled squares, and look nearly the same.
Our children will not know it's a different country.
All we can hope to leave them now is money.

1969

Philip Larkin

What the Chairman Told Tom

Poetry? It's a hobby.
I run model trains.
Mr Shaw there breeds pigeons.

It's not work. You dont sweat.
Nobody pays for it.
You *could* advertise soap.

Art, that's opera; or repertory –
The Desert Song.
Nancy was in the chorus.

But to ask for twelve pounds a week –
married, aren't you? –
you've got a nerve.

How could I look a bus conductor
in the face
if I paid you twelve pounds?

Who says it's poetry, anyhow?
My ten year old
can do it *and* rhyme.

I get three thousand and expenses,
a car, vouchers,
but I'm an accountant.

They do what I tell them,
my company.
What do *you* do?

Nasty little words, nasty long words,
it's unhealthy.
I want to wash when I meet a poet.

They're Reds, addicts,
all delinquents.
What you write is rot.

Mr Hines says so, and he's a schoolteacher,
he ought to know.
Go and find *work*.

Basil Bunting

SECURITIES

'O England –
hedge-bound as Larkin
omnivorous as Shakespeare.'
                    – Grace Nichols

1990s

Phrase Book

I'm standing here inside my skin,
which will do for a Human Remains Pouch
for the moment. Look down there (up here).
Quickly. Slowly. This is my front room

where I'm lost in the action, live from a war,
on screen. I am an Englishwoman, I don't understand you.
What's the matter? You are right. You are wrong.
Things are going well (badly). Am I disturbing you?

TV is showing bliss as taught to pilots:
Blend, Low silhouette, Irregular shape, Small,
Secluded. (Please write it down. Please speak slowly.)
Bliss is how it was in this very room

when I raised my body to his mouth,
when he even balanced me in the air,
or at least I thought so and yes the pilots say
yes they have caught it through the Side-Looking

Airborne Radar, and through the J-Stars.
I am expecting a gentleman (a young gentleman,
two gentlemen, some gentlemen). Please send him
(them) up at once. This is really beautiful.

Yes they have seen us, the pilots, in the Kill Box
on their screens, and played the routine for
getting us Stealthed, that is, Cleansed, to you and me,
Taken Out. They know how to move into a single room

like that, to send in with Pinpoint Accuracy, a hundred Harms.
I have two cases and a cardboard box. There is another
bag there. I cannot open my case – look out,
the lock is broken. Have I done enough?

Bliss, the pilots say, is for evasion
and escape. What's love in all this debris?
Just one person pounding another into dust,
into dust. I do not know the word for it yet.

Where is the British Consulate? Please explain.
What does it mean? What must I do? Where
can I find? What have I done? I have done
nothing. Let me pass please. I am an Englishwoman

Jo Shapcott

1950s

Afternoon Tea

She poured the tea. Vaguely I watched her hands.
The mask was fitted: in my wandering dream
Were boulder-broken valleys, a strange land.
Remote, astonished, I stood by a stream
Holding her hand in mine. The afternoon
Moved in my bones. Sun flecked the leaves and sand.
And she seemed fragile: but with roots in stone,
Blue-veined, the flower of a northern land.

And then things changed: and do not ask me why:
But privately and gently, as her hand
Might let mine fall, all love became a lie:
My gesture broke upon a dream beyond
Scones and my witty mouth and those chic cups
And the strange look that fussed me into rhyme:
An inarticulate wincing at the lips:
At last the key: and I came back to Time.

There to achieve a root, slowly to grow,
Is all my will. Here no one can elude
Desire, but in this city, when I go,
I'll leave a bedtime and destructive mood.
Her anger dwells there, wistful; and my drouth
Burns in the shadow country of a dream
Where her cool mouth flows backward from my mouth
And her long hands sustain a golden stream.

Dom Moraes

Eunice

With her latest roses happily encumbered
   Tunbridge Wells Central takes her from the night,
Sweet second bloomings frost has faintly umbered
   And some double dahlias waxy red and white.

Shut again till April stands her little hutment
   Peeping over daisies Michaelmas and mauve,
Lock'd is the Elsan in its brick abutment
   Lock'd the little pantry, dead the little stove.

Keys with Mr Groombridge, but nobody will take them
   To her lonely cottage by the lonely oak,
Potatoes in the garden but nobody to bake them,
   Fungus in the living room and water in the coke.

I can see her waiting on this chilly Sunday
   For the five forty (twenty minutes late),
One of many hundreds to dread the coming Monday
   To fight with influenza and battle with her weight.

Tweed coat and skirt that with such anticipation
   On a merry spring time a friend had trimm'd with fur,
Now the friend is married and, oh desolation,
   Married to the man who might have married *her*.

High in Onslow Gardens where the soot flakes settle
   An empty flat is waiting her struggle up the stair
And when she puts the wireless on, the heater and the kettle
   It's cream and green and cosy, but home is never there.

Home's here in Kent and how many morning coffees
   And hurried little lunch hours of planning will be spent
Through the busy months of typing in the office
   Until the days are warm enough to take her back to Kent.

John Betjeman

Wind

This house has been far out at sea all night,
The woods crashing through darkness, the booming hills,
Winds stampeding the fields under the window
Floundering black astride and blinding wet

Till day rose; then under an orange sky
The hills had new places, and wind wielded
Blade-light, luminous black and emerald,
Flexing like the lens of a mad eye.

At noon I scaled along the house-side as far as
The coal-house door. Once I looked up –
Through the brunt wind that dented the balls of my eyes
The tent of the hills drummed and strained its guyrope,

The fields quivering, the skyline a grimace,
At any second to bang and vanish with a flap;
The wind flung a magpie away and a black-
Back gull bent like an iron bar slowly. The house

Rang like some fine green goblet in the note
That any second would shatter it. Now deep
In chairs, in front of the great fire, we grip
Our hearts and cannot entertain book, thought,

Or each other. We watch the fire blazing,
And feel the roots of the house move, but sit on,
Seeing the window tremble to come in,
Hearing the stones cry out under the horizons.

Ted Hughes

Watercolour of Grantchester Meadows

There, spring lambs jam the sheepfold. In air
Stilled, silvered as water in a glass
Nothing is big or far.
The small shrew chitters from its wilderness
Of grassheads and is heard.
Each thumb-size bird
Fits nimble-winged in thickets, and of good colour.

Cloudrack and owl-hollowed willows slanting over
The bland Granta double their white and green
World under the sheer water
And ride that flux at anchor, upside down.
The punter sinks his pole.
In Byron's pool
Cat-tails part where the tame cygnets steer.

It is a country on a nursery plate.
Spotted cows revolve their jaws and crop
Red clover or gnaw beetroot
Bellied on a nimbus of sun-glazed buttercup.
Hedging meadows of benign
Arcadian green
The blood-berried hawthorn hides its spines with white.

Droll, vegetarian, the water rat
Saws down a reed and swims from his limber grove,
While the students stroll or sit,
Hands laced, in a moony indolence of love –
Black-gowned, but unaware
How in such mild air
The owl shall stoop from his turret, the rat cry out.

Sylvia Plath

The Pot Geranium

Green slated gables clasp the stem of the hill
In the lemony autumn sun; an acid wind
Dissolves the leaf-stalks of back-garden trees,
And chimneys with their fires unlit
Seem yet to puff a yellow smoke of poplars.
Freestone is brown as bark, and the model bakery
That once was a Primitive Methodist Chapel
Lifts its cornice against the sky.
And now, like a flight of racing pigeons
Slipped from their basket in the station yard,
A box-kite rides the air, a square of calico,
Crimson as the cornets of the Royal Temperance Band
When they brass up the wind in marching. The kite
Strains and struggles on its leash, and unseen boys,
In chicken run or allotment or by the side
Of the old quarry full to the gullet with water,
Pay out on their string a rag of dream,
High as the Jubilee flagpole.
                    I turn from the window
(Letting the bobbins of autumn wind up the swallows)
And lie on my bed. The ceiling
Slopes over like a tent, and white walls
Wrap themselves round me, leaving only
A flap for the light to blow through. Thighs and spine
Are clamped to the mattress and looping springs
Twine round my chest and hold me. I feel the air
Move on my face like spiders, see the light
Slide across the plaster; but wind and sun
Are mine no longer, nor have I kite to claim them,
Or string to fish the clouds. But there on a shelf
In the warm corner of my dormer window
A pot geranium flies its bright balloon,

Nor can the festering hothouse of the tropics
Breed a tenser crimson; for this crock of soil,
Six inch deep by four across,
Contains the pattern, the prod and pulse of life,
Complete as the Nile or the Niger.
               And what need therefore
To stretch for the straining kite? For kite and flower
Bloom in my room for ever; the light that lifts them
Shines in my own eyes, and my body's warmth
Hatches their red in my veins. It is the Gulf Stream
That rains down the chimney, making the soot spit; it is the
    Trade Wind
That blows in the draught under the bedroom door.
My ways are circumscribed, confined as a limpet
To one small radius of rock; yet
I eat the equator, breathe the sky, and carry
The great white sun in the dirt of my fingernails.

Norman Nicholson

The Balloon at Selborne

'At twenty minutes before three there
was a cry – the balloon was come.'
> – *Letters of Gilbert White*

Into the silk blue sky it sails,
A sphere, netted like an overripe plum.
The dangling birdcage basket trembles.
The villagers are stricken dumb,

And Parson White, his hat in hand
Watches as if a rare bird flew.
Under his feet, the orchis, unheeded
Lies trampled, rotting in a grave of dew.

Over the grass, the lobbed, dark shadow
Dips and veers; the frightened sheep
Run and huddle and stare as it harries them.
Over the Hangar's green-fleeced steep

It spins and tacks and dwindles and is gone.
The sheep graze quietly; home amble the cottagers
To the wavering rushlight and mole-grey evening.
Blanchard in his basket nods to other villages,

Another day of summer withers and dies
Over western skies with its thorn-red stains.
But ah, now with it the innocence has gone.
Only the shadow on the grass remains.

Margaret Stanley-Wrench

Patriotic Poem

This mildewed island,
Rained on and beaten flat by bombs and water,
Seems ready now to crack like any other
Proud organism drugged with praise and torture.

History rolls
His heavy tide of insolence and wonder
Scarring her surface with as many holes
As her moth-eaten sky where fighters thunder.

Yet from the cauldron
Where her hard bones are formed by time and anguish
Rises the living breath of all her children;
And her deep heart and theirs, who can distinguish?

John Wain

A Ballad for Katharine of Aragon

Queen of England, 1509–33
Buried in Peterborough Cathedral

As I walked down by the river
Down by the frozen fen
I saw the grey cathedral
With the eyes of a child of ten.
O the railway arch is smoky
As the Flying Scot goes by
And but for the Education Act
Go Jumper Cross and I.

But war is a bitter bugle
That all must learn to blow
And it didn't take long to stop the song
In the dirty Italian snow.
O war is a casual mistress
And the world is her double bed.
She has a few charms in her mechanised arms
But you wake up and find yourself dead.

The olive tree in winter
Casts her banner down
And the priest in white and scarlet
Comes up from the muddy town.
O never more will Jumper
Watch the Flying Scot go by.
His funeral knell was a six-inch shell
Singing across the sky.

The Queen of Castile has a daughter
Who won't come home again.
She lies in the grey cathedral
Under the arms of Spain.
O the Queen of Castile has a daughter
Torn out by the roots,
Her lovely breast in a cold stone chest
Under the farmers' boots.

Now I like a Spanish party
And many O many's the day
I have watched them swim as the night came dim
In Algeciras Bay.
O the high sierra was thunder
And the seven-branched river of Spain
Came down to the sea to plunder
The heart of the sailor again.

O shall I leap in the river
And knock upon paradise door
For a gunner of twenty-seven and a half
And a queen of twenty-four?
From the almond tree by the river
I watch the sky with a groan,
For Jumper and Kate are always out late
And I lie here alone.

Charles Causley

I Remember

It was my bridal night I remember,
An old man of seventy-three
I lay with my young bride in my arms,
A girl with t.b.
It was wartime, and overhead
The Germans were making a particularly heavy raid on Hampstead.
What rendered the confusion worse, perversely
Our bombers had chosen that moment to set out for Germany.
Harry, do they ever collide?
I do not think it has ever happened,
Oh my bride, my bride.

Stevie Smith

Leaving England

I have hardly set foot upon your soil,
silent land, hardly touched one stone,
so high into your sky was I lifted
so taken up by the clouds, haze, and beyond
that I had already left you
as I dropped anchor.

You fastened my eyes
with sea breath, oak touch,
you tapped my miseries
to keep the grasses lush;
exploring, each dream sun
released from my head
found everything had gone
once your day started.
Everything remained unsaid.

Along the lanes flutter the great grey birds
and drive me out.
Was I ever here?

I didn't want to be observed.

My eyes are open.
Sea breath, oak touch?
Under the ocean's coils
I see in your place, crushed,
the country of my soul.

I have never set foot upon its soil.

Ingeborg Bachmann,
translated from the German by John Greening

VISIONARY

'All
That has passed this way is magical
No wonder therefore if the light
Falls upon England tonight
Extenuating what is ill.'

— *C.H. Sisson*

2000s

A Vision

The future was a beautiful place, once.
Remember the full-blown balsa-wood town
on public display in the Civic Hall?
The ring-bound sketches, artists' impressions,

blueprints of smoked glass and tubular steel,
board-game suburbs, modes of transportation
like fairground rides or executive toys.
Cities like *dreams*, cantilevered by light.

And people like us at the bottle bank
next to the cycle path, or dog-walking
over tended strips of fuzzy-felt grass,
or model drivers, motoring home in

electric cars. Or after the late show –
strolling the boulevard. They were the plans,
all underwritten in the neat left hand
of architects – a true, legible script.

I pulled that future out of the north wind
at the landfill site, stamped with today's date,
riding the air with other such futures,
all unlived in and now fully extinct.

Simon Armitage

1940s

from *Little Gidding*

Midwinter spring is its own season
Sempiternal though sodden towards sundown,
Suspended in time, between pole and tropic.
When the short day is brightest, with frost and fire,
The brief sun flames the ice, on pond and ditches,
In windless cold that is the heart's heat,
Reflecting in a watery mirror
A glare that is blindness in the early afternoon.
And glow more intense than blaze of branch, or brazier,
Stirs the dumb spirit: no wind, but pentecostal fire
In the dark time of the year. Between melting and freezing
The soul's sap quivers. There is no earth smell
Or smell of living thing. This is the spring time
But not in time's covenant. Now the hedgerow
Is blanched for an hour with transitory blossom
Of snow, a bloom more sudden
Than that of summer, neither budding nor fading,
Not in the scheme of generation.
Where is the summer, the unimaginable
Zero summer?

        If you came this way,
Taking the route you would be likely to take
From the place you would be likely to come from,
If you came this way in may time, you would find the hedges
White again, in May, with voluptuary sweetness.
It would be the same at the end of the journey,
If you came at night like a broken king,

If you came by day not knowing what you came for,
It would be the same, when you leave the rough road
And turn behind the pig-sty to the dull façade
And the tombstone. And what you thought you came for
Is only a shell, a husk of meaning
From which the purpose breaks only when it is fulfilled
If at all. Either you had no purpose
Or the purpose is beyond the end you figured
And is altered in fulfilment. There are other places
Which also are the world's end, some at the sea jaws,
Or over a dark lake, in a desert or a city –
But this is the nearest, in place and time,
Now and in England.

T.S. Eliot

A Room at Nightfall

As England's earth moves into dark, the fire is painted,
Shines like speech in the dulled room.
Nocturnal lights of man come out in streets and windows
And cars heard passing. Last to bloom
Of all lights, the narcissus-white lamp on our table
Flowers at a touch, is shaken wide;
And far the sky, Eurydice, falls back, the house-roofs,
Night trees are emptied. We inside
Seem to hang in a domed pearl where light with shadow,
Shadow is interfused with light.
Draw the curtains, perfect the moon-round, moon-coloured
Globe that hangs so still in night.

E.J. Scovell

Daybreak

Morning is a revealing; confession of rivers,
Rainfall hushed of the rhetoric of surprise,
Field that can furrow the heart; a land our eyes
Have learnt by rote, not leaned over like lovers;

Secret divulged, of towns in a pit of horror,
Wars white-hot in the foundry's flickering womb;
Compassionately day underlines the doom
We paste on a hoarding, peer at in a mirror;

Tripped by the tree's root — all perfection felled
Yet faint with bloom – we flatter in man the torrid
Zealot of metal, cheat the wildwood forehead,
Prune of its green desire the desolate world.

Morning is a redeeming and a condemning.
Sparrows at two a farthing leave no smudge
On sanguine earth. May dawn forbear to judge
Between my blood-guilt and the bomber gleaming.

Lilian Bowes Lyon

Son of Mist

Mist is your mother, Englishman,
You were born out of the mist.
Her wisdom is an old woman's,
How to yield and how persist.

Your first morning was a struggle
Out of her clasp, and each
Morning of history is the same.
She is in your speech.

By tongue, eye, thought you came
Under her pliant rule.
Through her you saw house and tree
On your way to school.

River, spire and monument
Dawned out of her each day;
Mist on the quay and in your throat
When you steamed away.

Your life despaired of, you embarked
Knick-knacks and medicine-chest
Empiring through lands of sun,
A consumptive's quest;

Or worked at home and tried to learn
What she never taught,
To see the exact image, know
The unblurred thought.

Old, unageing, in wisdom blind
Your mother everywhere
Pervades her charming fields content
Not knowing your despair.

James Reeves

Wensleydale

Today all things compose
A magical incantation:
From change or death immune
The leopard in the hedge
Is dappled with the rose,
And just beyond Sight, Imagination
An eagle from the sun
Stoops from his golden ledge.

Bird, fish, animal,
The witness of the hills
Whose testament is mute,
The lissom river's length –
All the enchanting dale
Within the heart and mind distils
Its creatures form and fruit,
Its superhuman strength.

You can spread out a map
And say the Dale is spread;
The hill's a contour-line
And the river is a word:
As from the subtlest trap
You get at most the living dead,
A cold and empty skin
Or a stuffed singing bird.

Men to each other are
Maps read in curtained rooms,
And human intercourse
By conventional sign and scale

Can only go so far –
Until the sudden traveller comes
Who folds the map and goes
Into the magic dale.

There is the land that plays
Chameleon to the weather,
There curlew upon the scree
Or trout sleek in the pool
By natural synthesis
Fulfil the body and soul together
And life in every key
Is right and beautiful.

Compass and Map are gone
For Love must needs destroy
All things vicarious:
He has the measure of
The soul and the skeleton,
Yet his immeasurable joy
By flesh and blood is ours,
Is ours, is now, my love.

Patric Dickinson

The Island City

for R.J.S.

Walking among this island
People inhabiting this island city,
Whose coast recedes, whose facile sand
Bears cold cathedrals restively:
I see a black time coming, history
Tending in footnotes our forgotten land.

Hearing the once-virginal
But ageing choirs of intellect
Sing a psalm that would appal
Our certain fathers, I expect
No gentle decadence, no right effect
Of falling, but itself the barren fall:
And Yeats' gold songbird shouting over all.

Sidney Keyes

In the Backs

Too many of the dead, some I knew well,
Have smelt this unforgotten river smell,
Liquid and old and dank;
And on the tree-dark, lacquered, slowly passing stream
Have seen the boats come softly as in dream
Past the green bank.
So Camus, reverend sire, came footing slow
Three hundred years ago,
And Milton paced the avenue of trees
In miracle of sun and shade as now,
The fresh-attempted glorious cadences
Behind his youthful brow.

Milton and Chaucer, Herbert, Herrick, Gray,
Rupert, and you forgotten others, say –
Are there slow rivers and bridges where you have gone away?
What has your spirit found?
What wider lot?
Some days in spring do you come back at will,
And tread with weightless feet the ancient ground?
O say, if not,
Why is this air so sacred and so still?

Frances Cornford

Voices

I heard those voices today again:
Voices of women and children, down in that hollow
Of blazing light into which swoops the tree-darkened lane
Before it mounts up into the shadow again.

I turned the bend – just as always before
There was no one at all down there in the sunlit hollow;
Only ferns in the wall, foxgloves by the hanging door
Of that blind old desolate cottage. And just as before

I noticed the leaping glitter of light
Where the stream runs under the lane; in that mine-dark archway
– Water and stones unseen as though in the gloom of night –
Like glittering fish slithers and leaps the light.

I waited long at the bend of the lane,
But heard only the murmuring water under the archway.
Yet I tell you, I've been to that place again and again,
And always, in summer weather, those voices are plain,
Down near that broken house, just where the tree-darkened lane
Swoops into the hollow of light before mounting to shadow again…

Frances Bellerby

The Country House

Platonic, shadowed lawn,
Cooling airs, cradle of instinctive poise,
And memories of a richer age rippling like a shallow
Golden lake over the whole hedge-scented island:
There where the spry onanist sat in his Twickenham arbour
And hairy Wycherley bawled through the lace and periwigs
And the great pudding-faced Frenchman wrote, 'He who sets
       foot on the Dover shore has ceased to see life clearly!'

Which of them was the prophet? From Thurso to Penzance
And eastward to Lowestoft move the unequal mists,
Gently testifying to the stifling solaces of a tradition:
The widow sits knitting in the mossy cottage,
The weasel-eyed friend strolls down the lane with his spaniel,
And the silver tea service, left out under the starlight, and still
       as Everest, is gathering dew.

And now, the shadows deepen. Seventy odd
Curtains are drawn in the village. The radiant scythe
Moves closer through the crippled clouds: grows clear,
Hangs over the Menai straits and thorny Snowdon.
Wind pours past Anglesey through the channel. Birds,
Seabirds, millions of them, are flung westward in the net that
       circles over the shattering currents.

O England, England,
Land of the simmering teapot and articulate shadow,
Who knows what ears are listening to you now?
Who knows what apelike arm is ready to strike
Out of the Elizabethan wilderness, tearing
Open that awful flaw in the armour: imagination?

Clawing the vicar's studiously achieved security,
Prowling after the don's prim tread through the cloister,
Blurring the cricketer's perfect eye: all of them
Torn by a vision, not in the meditative refuge
For years so assiduously, dexterously cultivated,
But choking, spluttering, tremendous at last with meaning,
In the howling conflagration of the sea.

Frederic Prokosch

Journey to London

From the Welsh wick asleep in the globe of winter
I came across England to love and anger,
Came from that mountainous indifference
To where my hopes were, your lips, our danger.

Riding the three ranges, the high midland
Where history piled stone on stone together,
Furnishing from grey stone our politics
And the harsh principles that slay my brother,

Riding the three ranges, I left Malvern
In the flush of sunset and all Oxfordshire
To the veiled glory of its fabled spires,
Came down to darkness and a city's fear.

O London, from the pellucid flame of Wales,
I your citizen and twenty others
Crossed from the Chiltern daylight into darkness,
The night that drowns our enemies and lovers,

Journeyed from grey stone to bombs exploding
Our politics and prayers, to a new anger
Striking from war this poetry. I came
To the heart of love, to the heart of danger.

J.C. Hall

The Burning of the Leaves

Now is the time for the burning of the leaves.
They go to the fire; the nostril pricks with smoke
Wandering slowly into a weeping mist.
Brittle and blotched, ragged and rotten sheaves!
A flame seizes the smouldering ruin and bites
On stubborn stalks that crackle as they resist.

The last hollyhock's fallen tower is dust;
All the spices of June are a bitter reek,
All the extravagant riches spent and mean.
All burns! The reddest rose is a ghost;
Sparks whirl up, to expire in the mist: the wild
Fingers of fire are making corruption clean.

Now is the time for stripping the spirit bare,
Time for the burning of days ended and done,
Idle solace of things that have gone before:
Rootless hope and fruitless desire are there;
Let them go to the fire, with never a look behind.
The world that was ours is a world that is ours no more.

They will come again, the leaf and the flower, to arise
From squalor of rottenness into the old splendour,
And magical scents to a wondering memory bring;
The same glory, to shine upon different eyes.
Earth cares for her own ruins, naught for ours.
Nothing is certain, only the certain spring.

Laurence Binyon

POWER

'…and row as far as Totnes
and there get out and stand,
outcasts of the earth, kings
of the green island England.'
                    — *Alice Oswald*

2010s

Diagnosis: 'Londonism'

*a.k.a. Paging Dr Pangloss, you might need to
extend your rounds*

The panjandrum in his glass and steel lair
scans the wealth flowing across the river,
pulls up his chalkstripe pantaloons to declare:
you drones, we are not sick nor quivering.

The jobs are rich, filling and bountiful;
the inflation is flat and negligible,
the environment pleasingly perishable –
this economic model impregnable.

I know this because the bankers tell me so;
the politicians agree, then crow –
and my shoe leather is too precious
to walk beyond the green belt that chokes us.

I cannot help that I know more than you,
that my facts will always beat your facts,
because they come from gleaming technocrats,
the new look, new establishment crew.

Join me in celebrating this urban supremacy!
Embrace this rationalism so filigree!
What must we know of life beyond Zone 6?
It is a fine rumour, but does not exist.

Rishi Dastidar

1930s

The Pylons

The secret of these hills was stone, and cottages
Of that stone made,
And crumbling roads
That turned on sudden hidden villages.

Now over these small hills, they have built the concrete
That trails black wire;
Pylons, those pillars
Bare like nude giant girls that have no secret.

The valley with its gilt and evening look
And the green chestnut
Of customary root,
Are mocked dry like the parched bed of a brook.

But far above and far as sight endures
Like whips of anger
With lightning's danger
There runs the quick perspective of the future.

This dwarfs our emerald country by its trek
So tall with prophecy:
Dreaming of cities
Where often clouds shall lean their swan-white neck.

Stephen Spender

A Summer Night

To Geoffrey Hoyland

Out on the lawn I lie in bed,
Vega conspicuous overhead
    In the windless nights of June,
As congregated leaves complete
Their day's activity; my feet
    Point to the rising moon.

Lucky, this point in time and space
Is chosen as my working-place,
    Where the sexy airs of summer,
The bathing hours and the bare arms,
The leisured drives through a land of farms
    Are good to a newcomer.

Equal with colleagues in a ring
I sit on each calm evening
    Enchanted as the flowers
The opening light draws out of hiding
With all its gradual dove-like pleading,
    Its logic and its powers:

That later we, though parted then,
May still recall these evenings when
    Fear gave his watch no look;
The lion griefs loped from the shade
And on our knees their muzzles laid,
    And Death put down his book.

Now north and south and east and west
Those I love lie down to rest;
    The moon looks on them all,
The healers and the brilliant talkers,
The eccentrics and the silent walkers,
    The dumpy and the tall.

She climbs the European sky,
Churches and power stations lie
    Alike among earth's fixtures:
Into the galleries she peers
And blankly as a butcher stares
    Upon the marvellous pictures.

To gravity attentive, she
Can notice nothing here, though we
    Whom hunger does not move,
From gardens where we feel secure
Look up and with a sigh endure
    The tyrannies of love:

And, gentle, do not care to know,
Where Poland draws her eastern bow,
    What violence is done,
Nor ask what doubtful act allows
Our freedom in this English house,
    Our picnics in the sun.

Soon, soon, through the dykes of our content
The crumpling flood will force a rent,
    And, taller than a tree,
Hold sudden death before our eyes
Whose river dreams long hid the size
    And vigours of the sea.

But when the waters make retreat
And through the black mud first the wheat
  In shy green stalks appears;
When stranded monsters gasping lie,
And sounds of riveting terrify
  Their whorled unsubtle ears,

May these delights we dread to lose,
This privacy, need no excuse
  But to that strength belong,
As through a child's rash happy cries
The drowned parental voices rise
  In unlamenting song.

After discharges of alarm
All unpredicted let them calm
  The pulse of nervous nations;
Forgive the murderer in his glass,
Tough in its patience to surpass
  The tigress her swift motions.

W.H. Auden

After the Jubilee, 1935

The arches are down, the standards down, the flags have gone to store,
The pageants are done, and all the fun, and ceased the nightly roar,
And king and peasant must back to work, back to desk and plough,
There's no more time for rhythm and rhyme but that of the engines now.
But the tabard and gloves and the golden mail of Edward the Splendid Prince
Still guard his tomb as they've guarded it, all these centuries since;
Since the Pilgrimage met at the Southwark Inn, from cloister, hovel and hall,
And Chaucer rode at the Bath Wife's side, and watched, and smiled at it all.

Guards and Lancers, dragoons, hussars, they rode the streets in state,
Gold and scarlet and helm and plume that never were seen of late,
In the days of mud-coloured soldiery, and death that drops in the night;
They were seen, they are gone, like a glimpse of the past, they are hidden
    from the light;
But none can rob us of Nelson's hat, or his star or his armless sleeve
Where the clouds fly past and the birds fly round, morning and noon and eve:
And Wellington's horse stands proud on its base that Alfred Stevens made
Though the poison gas has reeked in the air and the deathless charges fade.

The problems press on the statesmen, they never know where to turn,
They never can look to East or West but something seems to burn,
A spark or a glow or an angry blaze that threatens at once to spread
Like a prairie fire for a thousand miles and envelop a thousand dead;
Yet were there no perils ere we were born, are we the first to shrink
From a vision of last disasters and a world gone over the brink?
Sidney died at Zutphen and Raleigh lies at the Tower
And Drake went down with the shot at his feet when England was in flower.

The streets swarm out and the woods are cut and the fields go down to grass
And all the ills that Cobbett cursed have grimly come to pass;
We struggle and struggle in webs of Fate, we strive to save the soul,

Soul and body and sense and dream in a world beyond control –
And the brave are all bewildered, and the cowards content to be sad,
But Shakespeare laughed with such knowledge of life as no man ever had
And still, whatever the chemists may brew, and the men who add the sums,
Though the mean malign and the pampered pine, there are flags in the
    heart of the slums.

John Squire

Children of wealth

Children of wealth in your warm nursery,
Set in the cushioned window-seat to watch
The volleying snow, guarded invisibly
By the clear double pane through which no touch
Untimely penetrates, you cannot tell
What winter means; its cruel truths to you
Are only sound and sight; your citadel
Is safe from feeling, and from knowledge too.

Go down, go out to elemental wrong,
Waste your too round limbs, tan your skin too white;
The glass of comfort, ignorance, seems strong
Today, and yet perhaps this very night

You'll wake to horror's wrecking fire – your home
Is wired within for this, in every room.

Elizabeth Daryush

from *Autumn Journal*

We lived in Birmingham through the slump –
　　Line your boots with a piece of paper –
Sunlight dancing on the rubbish dump,
　　On the queues of men and the hungry chimneys.
And the next election came –
　　Labour defeats in Erdington and Aston;
And life went on – for us went on the same;
　　Who were we to count the losses?
Some went back to work and the void
　　Took on shape while others climbing
The uphill nights of the unemployed
　　Woke in the morning to factory hooters.
Little on the plate and nothing in the post;
　　Queue in the rain or try the public
Library where the eye may coast
　　Columns of print for a hopeful harbour.
But roads ran easy, roads ran gay
　　Clear of the city and we together
Could put on tweeds for a getaway
　　South or west to Clee or the Cotswolds;
Forty to the gallon; into the green
　　Fields in the past of English history;
Flies in the bonnet and dust on the screen
　　And no look back to the burning city.
That was then and now is now,
　　Here again on a passing visit,
Passing through but how
　　Memory blocks the passage.
Just as in Nineteen-Thirty-One
　　Sun shines easy but I no longer

Docket a place in the sun –
    No wife, no ivory tower, no funk-hole.
The night grows purple, the crisis hangs
    Over the roofs like a Persian army
And all of Xenophon's parasangs
    Would take us only an inch from danger.
Black-out practice and ARP,
    Newsboys driving a roaring business,
The flapping paper snatched to see
    If anything has, or has not, happened.
And I go to the Birmingham Hippodrome
    Packed to the roof and primed for laughter
And beautifully at home
    With the ukulele and the comic chestnuts;
'As pals we meet, as pals we part' –
    Embonpoint and a new tiara;
The comedian spilling the apple-cart
    Of doubles entendres and doggerel verses
And the next day begins
    Again with alarm and anxious
Listening to bulletins
    From distant, measured voices
Arguing for peace
    While the zero hour approaches,
While the eagles gather and the petrol and oil and grease
    Have all been applied and the vultures back the eagles.
But once again
    The crisis is put off and things look better
And we feel negotiation is not vain –
    Save my skin and damn my conscience.
And negotiation wins,
    If you can call it winning,
And here we are – just as before – safe in our skins;

Glory to God for Munich.
And stocks go up and wrecks
   Are salved and politicians' reputations
Go up like Jack-on-the-Beanstalk; only the Czechs
   Go down and without fighting.

Louis MacNeice

Searchlights and Bombers

Lovers on the Heath lie, and raise
their heads and see the moon riding
this white and yellow ledge
of a brown bulk of cloud.

What sounds they catch are the
domestic hum of London, the crake
of a tram, brakes, a mallard,
another voice and their own

Emotional breathing: and coming,
coming now, the hum of Europe
above the wagging fingers of our end
on this brown bulk of cloud.

Geoffrey Grigson

Instructions from England, 1936

Note nothing of why or how, enquire
no deeper than you need
into what set these veins on fire,
note simply that they bleed.
Spain fought before and fights again,
better no question why;
note churches burned and popes in pain
but not the men who die.

Valentine Ackland

Now as Then

September 1939

When under Edward or Henry the English armies
Whose battles are brocade to us and stiff in tapestries
On a green and curling sea set out for France,
The Holy Ghost moved the sails, the lance
Was hung with glory, and in all its sincerity
    Poets cried 'God will grant to us the victory.'
For us, who by proxy inflicted gross oppression,
Among whom the humblest have some sins of omission,
War is not simple; in more or less degree
All are guilty, though some will suffer unjustly.
Can we say Mass to dedicate our bombs?
Yet those earlier English, for all their psalms,
Were marauders, had less provocation than we,
And the causes of war were as mixed and hard to see.
Yet since of two evils our victory would be the less,
And coming soon, leave some strength for peace,
Like Minot and the rest, groping we pray
    'Lord, turn us again, confer on us victory.'

Anne Ridler

The Silent Sunday

From the bandstand in the garden on the hill
Where workless seamen moped on benches
And shrieking children worked the swings
The wide curve of the estuary can be seen.

Halfway down the hill a murder case
Once drew idle crowds to stare
Over the mottled laurels in the garden of an inn,
And a newspaper stood up on end
And moved unsteadily, urged by the wind,
Like a child that learns to walk.

That busy world of cars and bungalows,
Who would have thought that it would stop so soon?
Fissures appeared in football fields
And houses in the night collapsed.
The Thames flowed backward to its source,
The last trickle seen to disappear
Swiftly, like an adder to its hole,
And here and there along the riverbed
The stranded fish gaped among empty tins;
Face downward lay the huddled suicides
Like litter that a riot leaves.

They say some women lived for weeks
Hidden in bushes on the common, then drew lots
And ate each other. Now
A sunny mist hangs over everything.
An almond tree suggests that this is spring
But on the right an oak retains its leaves.

Where are the sea birds? Why no gulls?
All drowned when the oil-tanks burst?
Water chuckles from a broken pipe.

William Plomer

The Eight Men

The tower is silent as we mount,
Except for the ancestral clock
Who clucks a little iron tongue
Each second of time, as he has done
For twenty generations to count
In drops of baptism, and the knock
Of earth on coffin, one by one —
Life unwinding, life outspun.

Shuffle of leather on the stone;
A feather-quilted bird who wakes
And shakes a wing, that makes alone
A little fury in the quill
And then subsides. All is still.

Round by round, the belfry stair
Falls below us; through the slit
We see a winter world, moonlit;
Midnight roofs, trees black and bare,
A horse who breathes the silver air
Beside the graveyard wall. And then
Eight friendly, local Englishmen,
All of one parish, doff their coats,
Set down the lantern by the wall,
Husk a few words, and clear their throats,
Unknot the snaky ropes, and stand
Each with a demon under his hand,
His iron slave poised for the fall.

There is no other sound at all:
The bird sleeps, the trees outside
Finger the stars, and catch the white
Frost-fallings of the Christmastide,
But make no movement: far and wide
The fields are frozen; the rusty vane
Groans; then the world is quiet again.
Only the clock: 'Tick!... tock!... *tack*... tock!'

'Ready?' says the tenor; but none replies.
We wait, we are ready; eight pairs of eyes
Glance swift answer; eight arms lift.
'Then... go!' he shouts, and one by one
The eight arms swing down, and down
Bang the bells! The belfry holds
The fury, hollows itself and folds
The flood from clapper and rim, but soon
The tower is swimming, the octaves rise
On their own ringing selves and fling
Out and over the fields, the skies.
Even the silver frost, the hoar moon
Hum with their metal glint, the trees
Crook their fingers, pluck the stars
That ring out with their jewelled voices.
Hard echo upon salvo, back and forth
From High Piper to Tenor, mad Christian mirth
Half sinful with the pagan Earth,
Defying the silence of the spheres,
The frost, that ghost of Time, the fall
Of the eternal Light, all Powers unanswerable.

The old horse grazes by the churchyard wall.

Richard Church

ENDGAME

'England. I think some clear and simple thing eludes me'

– Peter Oswald

2020s

Lord of Misrule

for Ian Marchant

Throwing up at the result of that referendum
My hot graffiti dripping from Parliament
   I bequeath thee shitte
Spamming every feed and trending now
The remedy, I say to the tired Christ
Slack in my skin
Is to be drunk, 'on wine, poetry or virtue, as you wish'
Preferably all three at once.
O for some Weimar easy virtue, given wisely
To snuff the insolence of office out
And dance a tango
Through their sober death.
I mean to teach these suits morality.

After a dunk in the Thames, black as oil,
I board my Zeppelin.
Far below, the city streets are floes of fire.
Pepys runs to bury his wheel of Parmesan cheese.
He, at least, takes my advice.

You are invited to the Feast of Fools.
Come dressed as the century,
Each of you a prophecy.
I will supply a little theatre.

Pale mummers, their tongues all told,
Haunt year zero:
Remind you that the dead can live
And will perform for food.
Will Kemp in his cap and bells
Dances a morris to Primal Scream
And conjures a crocus from broken earth.

The homeless, housed in Kensington
Drop pennies into the cups of royal rough sleepers
Cold on their thrones.
Those who once made money out of money
Even in 'crisis'
Find life in laying a hedge of hazel and willow
In the Midlands style.
I thought er wuz jed, one says, audible
Tears in the voice he has found in his blood.
I thought er wuz jed, an the spudgucks n'all
But they ay, they ay
Er's in this wand, an the spudgucks n'all.

Our revels last three days of night.
The players breed with the crowd.
When at last the lights go out
I let a full breast slip from my dress,
Dance with the living and the dead
Our mouths at our necks
Until Albion shudders its *petite mort.*

The suits drop their jaws, enlightened.

Shh. Go easy on that hungover head.
There are those who would hang us by an ankle
Until we bleed dry.

I play myself as a Tarot card
To see their fear eye to eye.

They will trespass at dawn
To drag me from my enseamèd bed
In the name of the crime they've dressed as the law
And ungratefully frame my jest as offence.
Someone will shout: My poor fool is hanged
But I will wink
From the gallows
When they think
I am dead.

Gregory Leadbetter

1920s

from *The Waste Land*

The river's tent is broken; the last fingers of leaf
Clutch and sink into the wet bank. The wind
Crosses the brown land, unheard. The nymphs are departed.
Sweet Thames, run softly, till I end my song.
The river bears no empty bottles, sandwich papers,
Silk handkerchiefs, cardboard boxes, cigarette ends
Or other testimony of summer nights. The nymphs are departed.
And their friends, the loitering heirs of City directors;
Departed, have left no addresses.
By the waters of Leman I sat down and wept…
Sweet Thames, run softly till I end my song,
Sweet Thames, run softly, for I speak not loud or long.
But at my back in a cold blast I hear
The rattle of the bones, and chuckle spread from ear to ear.

T.S. Eliot

Innocent England

Oh what a pity, Oh! don't you agree
that figs aren't found in the land of the free!

Fig trees don't grow in my native land;
there's never a fig leaf near at hand

when you want one; so I did without;
and that is what the row's about.

Virginal, pure policemen came
and hid their faces for very shame,

while they carried the shameless things away
to gaol, to be hid from the light of day.

And Mr Mead, that old, old lily
said: 'Gross! coarse! hideous!' – and I, like a silly,

thought he meant the faces of the police-court officials,
and how right he was, and I signed my initials

to confirm what he said; but alas, he meant
my pictures, and on the proceedings went.

The upshot was, my pictures must burn
that English artists might finally learn

when they painted a nude, to put a *cache sexe* on,
a cache sexe, a cache sexe, or else begone!

A fig leaf; or, if you cannot find it
a wreath of mist, with nothing behind it.

A wreath of mist is the usual thing
in the north, to hide where the turtles sing.

Though they never sing, they never sing,
don't you dare to suggest such a thing

or Mr Mead will be after you.
– But what a pity I never knew

a wreath of English mist would do
as a cache sexe! I'd have put a whole fog.

But once and forever barks the old dog,
so my pictures are in prison, instead of in the Zoo.

D.H. Lawrence

In the National Gallery

Faces irresolute and unperplexed –
Unspeculative faces, bored and weak,
Cruise past each patient victory of technique
Dimly desiring to enjoy the next
Yet never finding what they seem to seek.

Here blooms, recedes, and glows before their eyes
A quintessential world preserved in paint,
Calm vistas of long-vanished Paradise,
And ripe remembrances of sage and saint;
The immortality of changeless skies,
And all bright legendries of Time's creation…
    Yet I observe no gestures of surprise
    From those who straggle in to patronise
    The Art Collection of the English Nation.

Siegfried Sassoon

The Trees are Down

'And he cried with a loud voice, saying
Hurt not the Earth, neither the sea, nor the trees.'
                                        — *Revelation*

They are cutting down the great plane trees at the end of the gardens.
For days there has been the grate of the saw, the swish of the branches
    as they fall,
The crash of the trunks, the rustle of trodden leaves,
With the 'Whoops' and the 'Whoas', the loud common talk, the
    loud common laughs of the men, above it all.

I remember one evening of a long past Spring
Turning in at a gate, getting out of a cart, and finding a large dead
    rat in the mud of the drive.
I remember thinking: alive or dead, a rat was a god-forsaken thing,
But at least, in May, that even a rat should be alive.

The week's work here is as good as done. There is just one bough
        On the roped bole, in the fine grey rain,
                Green and high
                And lonely against the sky.
                    (Down now!—)
                And but for that,
                If an old dead rat
Did once, for a moment, unmake the Spring, I might never have
    thought of him again.

It is not for a moment the Spring is unmade today;
These were great trees, it was in them from root to stem:
When the men with the 'Whoops' and the 'Whoas' have carted the
    whole of the whispering loveliness away
Half the Spring, for me, will have gone with them.

It is going now, and my heart has been struck with the hearts of the planes;
Half my life it has beat with these, in the sun, in the rains,
          In the March wind, the May breeze,
In the great gales that came over to them across the roofs from the great seas.
          There was only a quiet rain when they were dying;
          They must have heard the sparrows flying,
And the small creeping creatures in the earth where they were lying –
          But I, all day, I heard an angel crying:
          'Hurt not the trees.'

Charlotte Mew

from *The Land (Winter)*

For now when fields beneath the wintry light
Lie stark, and snow along the hedgerow clings,
When streams of rooks on swerving wings
Blacken the sky with their untidy flight,
When iron ridges bind the frozen clay,
And sunset reddens cart ruts on the road –
Now in the wolf-month, shrammed and gaunt,
When vixens prowl, and hopping birds grow bold,
And craven otters haunt
The coops, by famine driven, and by cold –
There's little chance for labour on the land.
Only the dung cart with its reasty load
Creaks safe across the fields on frozen ground,
And horses for the fork or shovel stand
Patient, their nostrils smoking on the air.
Carting's a winter job. The strawy mound,
The wedge-shaped hale of roots for winter feeding stored,
Gapes, and gives up its rolling, orange hoard,
Cut in the farmyard troughs to equal share.
There's little else in these dead months to keep
The farm-folks brisk; at dawn and dusk they go
To break the ice on inky water-holes;
Fold on fresh patch of swedes the fattening sheep;
Put in a casual hour to dig out moles.
All desultory tasks, while the short day
Dulls from the morning's red to undern grey,
And dyes to red again as sun sinks low.

Vita Sackville-West

A Wish

I would hope for the children of West Ham
Wooden-frame houses square, with some-sort stuff
Crammed in to keep the wind away that's rough,
And rain; in summer cool, in cold comfortable enough.
Easily destroyed – and pretty enough, and yet tough.
Instead of brick and mortar tiled houses of no
Special appearance or attractive show.
Not crowded together, but with a plot of land,
Where one might play and dig, and use spade or the hand
In managing or shaping earth in such forms
As please the sunny mind or keep out of harms
The mind that's always good when let go its way
(I think) so there's work enough in a happy day.

Not brick and tile, but wood, thatch, walls of mixed
Material, and buildings in plain strength fixed.
Likeable, good to live in, easily pulled
Down, and in winter with warm ruddy light filled –
In summer with cool air; O better this sort of shelter –
And villages on the land set helter-skelter
On hillsides, dotted on plains – than the too exact
Straight streets of modern times, that strait and strict
And formal keep man's spirit within bounds,
Where too dull duties keep in monotonous rounds.

These villages to make for these towns of today –
O haste – and England shall be happy with the May
Or meadow-reach to watch, miles to see and away.

Ivor Gurney

Tell me not here...

Tell me not here, it needs not saying,
   What tune the enchantress plays
In aftermaths of soft September
   Or under blanching mays,
For she and I were long acquainted
   And I knew all her ways.

On russet floors, by waters idle,
   The pine lets fall its cone;
The cuckoo shouts all day at nothing
   In leafy dells alone;
And traveller's joy beguiles in autumn
   Hearts that have lost their own.

On acres of the seeded grasses
   The changing burnish heaves;
Or marshalled under moons of harvest
   Stand still all night the sheaves;
Or beeches strip in storms for winter
   And stain the wind with leaves.

Possess, as I possessed a season,
   The countries I resign,
Where over elmy plains the highway
   Would mount the hills and shine,
And full of shade the pillared forest
   Would murmur and be mine.

For nature, heartless, witless nature,
   Will neither care nor know
What stranger's feet may find the meadow

And trespass there and go,
Nor ask amid the dews of morning
  If they are mine or no.

A.E. Housman

Voices from Things Growing
in a Churchyard

These flowers are I, poor Fanny Hurd,
  Sir or Madam,
A little girl here sepultured.
Once I flit-fluttered like a bird
Above the grass, as now I wave
In daisy shapes above my grave,
  All day cheerily,
  All night eerily!

– I am one Bachelor Bowring, 'Gent',
  Sir or Madam;
In shingled oak my bones were pent;
Hence more than a hundred years I spent
In my feat of change from a coffin-thrall
To a dancer in green as leaves on a wall,
  All day cheerily,
  All night eerily!

– I, these berries of juice and gloss,
  Sir or Madam,
Am clean forgotten as Thomas Voss;
Thin-urned, I have burrowed away from the moss
That covers my sod, and have entered this yew,
And turned to clusters ruddy of view,
  All day cheerily,
  All night eerily!

– The Lady Gertrude, proud, high-bred,
  Sir or Madam,
Am I – this laurel that shades your head;

Into its veins I have stilly sped,
And made them of me; and my leaves now shine,
As did my satins superfine,
>> All day cheerily,
>> All night eerily!

— I, who as innocent withwind climb,
>> Sir or Madam,
Am one Eve Greensleeves, in olden time
Kissed by men from many a clime,
Beneath sun, stars, in blaze, in breeze,
As now by glowworms and by bees,
>> All day cheerily,
>> All night eerily!

— I'm old Squire Audeley Grey, who grew,
>> Sir or Madam,
Aweary of life, and in scorn withdrew;
Till anon I clambered up anew
As ivy-green, when my ache was stayed,
And in that attire I have longtime gayed
>> All day cheerily,
>> All night eerily!

— And so these maskers breathe to each
>> Sir or Madam
Who lingers there, and their lively speech
Affords an interpreter much to teach,
As their murmurous accents seem to come
Thence hitheraround in a radiant hum,
>> All day cheerily,
>> All night eerily!

Thomas Hardy

The Sad Shepherd

Of a day's motoring, of half England left behind,
Why should this one sight be so clear in my mind?
A country churchyard crowded with tombs and trees,
And three or four foot reared by the deaths of centuries,
So that we from the road could view as on a stage
The congregation coming out after morning prayer.
With loitering alacrity they trooped out into the air,
Greeting and grouping anew, glad to disengage
Voice and limb from decorum of Sunday demean,
Content to be going home, and content to have been.
But privily along a pathway narrow and overgrown
With hooding cypress the priest went walking alone,
Counter to the sun hastening, and away from his kind:
A black gown he wore and carried a book,
And I thought: There works some torment in that man's mind
Which he would hide from all, but which I by chance have seen –
For his lips were pinched close, and frenzy was in his look.

Sylvia Townsend Warner

As the team's head brass

As the team's head brass flashed out on the turn
The lovers disappeared into the wood.
I sat among the boughs of the fallen elm
That strewed an angle of the fallow, and
Watched the plough narrowing a yellow square
Of charlock. Every time the horses turned
Instead of treading me down, the ploughman leaned
Upon the handles to say or ask a word,
About the weather, next about the war.
Scraping the share he faced towards the wood,
And screwed along the furrow till the brass flashed
Once more.
          The blizzard felled the elm whose crest
I sat in, by a woodpecker's round hole,
The ploughman said. 'When will they take it away?'
'When the war's over.' So the talk began –
One minute and an interval of ten,
A minute more and the same interval.
'Have you been out?' 'No.' 'And don't want to, perhaps?'
'If I could only come back again, I should.
I could spare an arm. I shouldn't want to lose
A leg. If I should lose my head, why, so,
I should want nothing more... Have many gone
From here?' 'Yes.' 'Many lost?' 'Yes, a good few.
Only two teams work on the farm this year.
One of my mates is dead. The second day
In France they killed him. It was back in March,
The very night of the blizzard, too. Now if
He had stayed here we should have moved the tree.'
'And I should not have sat here. Everything
Would have been different. For it would have been

Another world.' 'Ay, and a better, though
If we could see all all might seem good.' Then
The lovers came out of the wood again:
The horses started and for the last time
I watched the clods crumble and topple over
After the ploughshare and the stumbling team.

Edward Thomas

EXIT HERE

'You cannot leave England, it turns
A planet majestically in the mind.'
                                    — *Peter Porter*

England, Where Did You Go?

England of the burrow-in green, the chalk-galvanised giant,
undulating earth-bank fortress, the flinted Roman wall,
the full-flair gorse, messy hay-trails waiting
to be bin-bag-baled by steel mandibles:

you unroll through the window of a train,
but should I get out in search of you, you'd be off,
and I'd be left wandering down dual carriageways,
looking across bean fields and filthy ditches.

Holly Hopkins

England

'Without nostalgia who could love England?'
— *Anne Stevenson*

Somewhere out there, England lingers
under the bushy brow of thatch that juts
above half-timbered houses in Home Counties.
A mill village survives where a raft
of flag irises rises near the grain loft
and the vicarage garden party is tastefully
announced on a hand-painted sign.
A family pile in Queen Anne style,
available at a knock-down price,
catches the needle-sharp eye
of a Lloyd's 'name' in the auction pages
of *The Field* or *Country Life*.
The hand-crafted. The home-made. The family-run.
Pink briar roses sink their claws
— like painted nails — into the gable walls
of listed cottages at Winchelsea and Rye.
Jersey cream dissolves in steaming scones
at the Salvation Army cake sale.
A smell of new-mown hay, of boiling jam,
of hops vented through an oast-house cowl.

England is still out there somewhere,
an owl roosting in a cobwebbed barn.
You can overhear a pub argument about
the best brew of beer, best-ever shepherd's pie.
Alistair Cooke is delivering his four millionth
'Letter from America'; so many record-breaking
West End performances of 'The Mousetrap' or 'Cats';

the ten thousandth revival of 'An Inspector Calls'.
Tin-plate, ration-coupon laughter from the audience
of a radio panel show; Lilliburlero marching
on the BBC World Service, Big Ben chiming
to the second with the tea-time news,
the sig tune for 'Coronation Street' a national anthem.
Johnners greets listeners from Lord's
as sunlight is rolled out along striped grass.
The tabloids have murder in their hearts.
That and exclusive photos of the latest
female tennis sensation at wet Wimbledon.
Scoreless draws in the Premier League.
Soft going at Newbury and Kempton Park.
Rain stopping play at a county cricket fixture.

Pastel-painted timber seaside chalets.
Miles of white clifftop caravans like dumped fridges.
A day-trip across ridged Channel waves:
cheap pints of bitter in the car ferry bar,
chips with everything in the cafeteria.
English Breakfast Served All Day in Calais.
Vera Lynn. VE celebrations. Our finest hour.
Poppy wreaths, brittle as old majors'
bones, wilt beneath the stony-faced
gaze of the Great War memorial.
Shakespeare settings by Roger Quilter
and Gerald Finzi in aid of the church tower
restoration fund, the vicar's wife doing
the page-turning needful for the accompanist.
A few tremble-lipped parishioners, feeling
their age, clear throats as the harmonium
is tuned and lend their bronchial best
to 'The Day Thou Gavest, Lord, is Ended'

while watery light through leaded glass
lands, like a housefly, on the brass plate
commemorating the valiant dead of Ladysmith.
Elgar's 'Pomp and Circumstance' arranged
for the Queen's visit by the colliery band.
Ralph Vaughan Williams's 'The Lark Ascending'
in rehearsal at the Free Trade Hall.
Gurney's Severn mists, Housman's blue
remembered hills, Hardy's wind and rain.
A Wilfred Owen troop train falling silent
at an unscheduled stop; or Edward Thomas's
halting express at Adlestrop taking on board
a consignment of pre-war blackbird song.
A brawny chestnut shields the clover-fattened
cattle in a hedgerowed field from searing noon.
Watercolour enthusiasts choose the ideal
viewing point to capture the flamboyant sunset.

The quiet courtesies. The moderation.
The pained smiles. Things left unsaid;
passed over in silence, an unwritten constitution.
Miles of graffitied tower blocks, near treeless
motorways wide as triumphal boulevards.
Race riots in Brixton and the North.
The peal of street-pleasing steel bands at Notting Hill.
Allotment cabbages with gaping caterpillar wounds.
Words like *tavern* and *shires* and *lea*.
Blazered Henley. Top-hatted Ascot.
Black herringbone for the Royal enclosure.
The wine-jacketed coach driver pointing
his blue-rinse passengers to the loos.
A single-room supplement for Christmas
at a refurbished Grand Hotel in some down-at-heel,
sea-eroded, once-genteel Edwardian town.

Romantic England is neither dead nor gone,
nor with Olivier in the grave.
It is out there somewhere still; plain-speaking
Stanley Baldwin's 'corncrake on a dewy morning,
the sound of the scythe against the whetstone…
a plough team coming over the brow of a hill'.
Homely John Major's England still holds its own
somewhere: 'long shadows on county grounds,
warm beer, invincible green suburbs, dog lovers'.
Goodly, portly Sir John Betjeman envisions his England:
'oil-lit churches, Women's Institutes, modest
village inns… mowing machines on Saturday afternoons'.

It is somewhere at the back of the mind,
like the back of a newsagent's where plug
tobacco is sold; shining like the polished
skin of a Ribston Pippin or Worcester Pearmain.
It preys on imagination, like pleated ladies
sporting on bowling lawns; like jowled men
of substance nursing claret in oak-panelled
smoking rooms of jovial private clubs.
See it all for yourself – the quadrangled choir school,
the parterred garden with the honesty box,
the fox-hunting colonel on his high horse,
the Gothic Revival haunt leading through
a topiary arch to gazebo, yew maze,
pet cemetery – on your jaunts about
cobbled market towns, treks down lanes
rutted with what surely must be hay wain wheels.

Listen to England as it thunders from Pennine becks
like a loud speech heckled by a Hyde Park crowd.
Listen to its screaming day traders, its bingo callers,
its Speaker demanding 'Order!' in the lower chamber.

Listen to the big band music to which couples
relax at the Conservative Club dinner dance.
Listen to the wax of silence harden
round the red leatherette upholstery
after closing time at the Crown and Rose;
steel shutters come down hard on the Punjab Balti;
grease congeals on the mobile kebab stall.
Listen to the tick of its Town Hall clocks,
like a Marks and Spencer shirt
drip-drying above a chipped enamel bath.
Listen to the silence in which England finds its voice.
It declaims this sceptred isle, this earth of majesty.
It claims some corner of a foreign field.
It chants while the chaffinch sings on the orchard bough.
It chants history is now and England.
It pleads green and pleasant land.
It pleads for all its many faults.

Dennis O'Driscoll

Being English

Farmers of Heathrow, my mother's family were Anglo-Saxon,
but for one Scottish great-grandmother to leaven the English.

My Jewish father, raised and schooled in Edinburgh,
left Scotland and Judaism. Did that make him English?

Hitler would think me Jewish enough, the Chief Rabbi
(should I ask him) wouldn't: default position – English.

I grew up in suburban Birmingham, my mixed blood
mingled with the soft Welsh water stolen by the English.

My language was delivered to me with the bottled milk
at the doorstep and at school. My greatest gift, my English.

This blessing entitles me to take it all for granted,
muttering under my breath at this land of the English.

Forgetfully arrogant, trying not to try too hard, proudly
we take up the cringe: pardon our empire, we're English.

Understatement and gentle irony, you say, have sunk us
under fair play and self-blame. We can be just 'too English'.

I'm afraid so – though, while you're saying it, the ones
who like to be disliked will be counting up who counts as English.

Bury me elsewhere if you must, but I can claim the earth
beneath Terminal 3: a place to welcome you in English.

Peter Daniels

A NOTE ON THE TEXT

The poems in this volume were selected during intensive and pleasurable consultation over two separate periods. While completing the editorial work on our anthology of English country houses, we realised we each had an interest in the more abstract topic of Englishness; a follow-up volume was proposed, and in the summer of 2021 we began gathering poems relating to Englishness. Initially, our search was unsystematic and desultory, as we had not yet hit on the organisational principle that would become *Contraflow*, and eventually the lack of a satisfactory structure caused us to drift from the project for a time until the idea suddenly coalesced in May, 2022.

Once we understood how we wanted to examine and present the idea of Englishness, we enjoyed a renewed burst of editorial creativity, and over the summer of 2022 we made all our final selections for the collection. Using both email and WhatsApp, we were able easily to share poems and lines we had each found. John has the larger library of niche contemporary poetry in his wooden 'word house' in Cambridgeshire, but Kevin has all the resources of a university in his Texas office, so between us we were able to do a fairly thorough trawl of possibilities.

The chosen poems were either written or first published in the allocated decade, but they do not all refer directly to that decade (e.g. Lorna Goodison's, recalling 1969 but published in 2005). Nevertheless, they are poems which emerged from the particular period, and so will to some extent reflect stylistic tendencies, which was one of the points of the anthology. We wanted to show how both English poetry and the sense of Englishness have developed over the last hundred years. The two opposing currents (and the riptides at the start and finish) would, we hope, stir up some new ways of understanding the century's poetry.

Some poems are excerpts from sequences or from longer poems. We have occasionally modernised punctuation (the use of comma and dash together) or silently corrected obvious typos. Although we have updated some archaic spellings, they cannot always be standardised, especially when poets disagree (luckily both Charles Causley and Penelope Shuttle opted for 'Katharine' of Aragon), or when they come from different cultures or were writing a hundred years ago. So American writers have been allowed to keep their preferred spellings, but among older writers we silently removed hyphens from such once-common compounds as 'week-end', 'good-bye', 'to-day', and 'half-way'. Even choice of punctuation can be tricky – as in Sylvia Plath's idiosyncratic use of the long dash, which we have retained. Where there has been any doubt about lineation we have either consulted the poets in question or checked against alternative editions. Where we've become aware that a poem was revised for a later edition, we've typically opted for the poet's final preferences for the poem. For instance, with Geoffrey Grigson's poem, 'Searchlights and Bombers' (originally titled 'The Bombers'), we use the retitled and lightly revised version, while situating the poem in the decade of its initial publication.

Alongside brief notes on the poets that follow, we have provided a few details about any facts or ambiguities in the poems. Information regarding original publication information for each poem, along with copyright permission statements, may be found in the 'Credits and Permissions' section.

JOHN GREENING & KEVIN GARDNER

NOTES ON THE POETS AND POEMS

Dannie Abse (1923–2014) He liked to write about his Welsh background, Jewishness and his life as a doctor, but London (he lived in Hampstead) also often featured in his poetry. His poem about the anti-Vietnam demonstration is a reminder that this distant war had a considerable impact on poetry in England.

Valentine Ackland (1906–69) Partner to Sylvia Townsend Warner, with whom she frequently collaborated. They lived together in rural Dorset, but Valentine (a pseudonym – she was born Kathleen) is remembered less for her often impressive poetry than for her personal life and communist sympathies.

Gillian Allnutt (1949–) Twice shortlisted for the T.S. Eliot Prize, she was awarded the Queen's Gold Medal in 2017. She grew up in the North-East, which features prominently in her uniquely spiritual, often minimalist poetry. Benwell is in Newcastle and was the scene of riots in 1991. The Armstrong mentioned was a celebrated Tyneside engineer and founder of Vickers Armstrong: he built houses for his workers, and the streets are allegedly named after his children (although, Allnutt tells us, 'he had none'). Dunston, Blaydon (home of the races) and the funfair Metroland lie just across the Tyne. A 'stottie' is a local flatbread.

Moniza Alvi (1954–) Brought to England from Pakistan at a young age, she grew up in Hertfordshire and settled in Wymondham, Norfolk. She has written about the tensions of immigrant life; her many collections are published by Bloodaxe.

The salwar kameez at the centre of her best-known poem is the Pakistani national dress, a traditional combination of trousers and long shirt, usually worn with a scarf.

Raymond Antrobus (1986–) Born in Hackney to an English mother and a Jamaican father, his deafness is just one of his themes. In 2019 he received the Rathbone Folio Prize and the Ted Hughes Award for new work; he has been shortlisted for several other major prizes. He is a gifted performer and in 2021 hosted a BBC radio documentary, *Inventions in Sounds*. Antrobus has been awarded an MBE and is a Fellow of the RSL.

Simon Armitage (1963–) Invariably drawn to 'All Points North' (the title of his memoir) and back to his native Yorkshire, he has written about the South-West Coast Path too. Even as Oxford Professor of Poetry and now Poet Laureate, the one-time probation officer has remained acutely aware of social divisions and is a witty observer of urban life.

W.H. Auden (1907–73) A man of the world, yet the limestone landscape of his Yorkshire childhood clearly mattered to him – his fissured features even came to resemble it. He defined a certain kind of garrulous, easy-going charm and natural facility which were perhaps better received abroad. Part of 'A Summer Night' (originally composed in June 1933 but we are using the later shortened version) was set by Britten in his *Spring Symphony*.

Ingeborg Bachmann (1926–73) This Austrian poet is considered one of the most enduring European poets of the mid-twentieth century. She was addicted to barbiturates, and probably died following severe burns in a fire caused by a cigarette. Her very inward-looking description of visiting (or not visiting) England is remarkable, given the post-war context.

Patricia Beer (1919–99) From a Plymouth Brethren family, she made her home in Devon and wrote extensively about the area, becoming one of the very few established women poets in the 60s and 70s. The West Country has been notoriously ill-served by railways, and Beeching's decision to cut branch lines was a severe blow and a deep sadness, well captured here (as also in Flanders & Swann's 'The Slow Train').

Frances Bellerby (1899–1975) Daughter of an Anglo-Catholic curate, she was brought up in a poor quarter of Bristol, worked as a maid, a teacher and eventually with a newspaper in London. She published a novel, volumes of short stories and six books of poetry, but suffered an accident in 1930 that left her crippled.

James Berry (1924–2017) He was a Jamaican poet who settled in London in the late 1940s (he worked for BT) becoming one of the first and most prominent Black writers in Britain, and a very influential anthologist. His work is fully represented in *A Story I Am In* (2011) but his 2007 book *Windrush Songs* is of particular significance.

Liz Berry (1980–) She is a poet whose work is rooted in the West Midlands. Her 2014 debut collection, *Black Country*, won a Somerset Maugham Award and the Geoffrey Faber Memorial Award as well as a Forward Prize. It contains many of her trademark dialect poems, which she performs inimitably. Subsequent books include *The Home Child*, a verse novel about the British Child Migrant Scheme.

John Betjeman (1906–84) His appreciation of all things English extended well beyond suburban London and his beloved home counties to the Cornwall of his childhood. As editor of the *Shell Guides* and a TV presenter he was spokesman on Englishness for several generations. In his poems, he might play with a brand name (rhyming on Drene and Innoxa in 'Middlesex', that Elsan lavatory in 'Eunice') or quote Tennyson and Blunden as in 'An Archaeological

Picnic'. He loved an obscure architectural term – 'Trans arcade' sounds today more exciting than it is, signifying a Transitional period when round and pointed arches were used together.

Laurence Binyon (1869–1943) Regularly quoted (and misquoted) on Remembrance Sunday, 'For the Fallen' is his most celebrated contribution to Englishness, yet Binyon was also an expert on Oriental art and Keeper of Prints and Drawings at the British Museum with a particular interest in Blake. The poem included here seems to be about the purgatorial effect of World War II.

Edmund Blunden (1896–1974) War poet, pastoralist, editor of neglected English writers and author of books about English places, he was from Yalding, Kent mattered hugely to him, as did Sussex, in whose regiment he fought. He was in Hong Kong and Japan for long stretches, but he lived latterly in Suffolk. The rural tradition is strong in 'Forefathers'.

Lilian Bowes Lyon (1895–1949) She was a cousin of King Charles III's grandmother. Very conscious of the gulf between rural Northumberland and sophisticated London, she contributed heroically to wartime voluntary work. She suffered from Buerger's Disease, losing her legs and the use of her hands. Her poetry received considerable recognition in the 30s and 40s.

Alison Brackenbury (1953–) She is a poet of rural England (Lincolnshire, where she grew up, and Gloucestershire, where she lives) and quirky Englishness, from its food to its mythology. Horses constantly trot through her poetry: her Selected was titled *Gallop* (2019).

Joseph Brodsky (1940–96) Expelled from the Soviet Union, he became an American and a popular figure in Britain, although his translations of his own work were not always well received. The poem here, translated by Alan Myers (and retaining its American spellings), is from a sequence 'In England'.

Basil Bunting (1900–85) From a Northumberland Quaker family, he rediscovered his roots after years abroad (and a series of verses on much more exotic subjects) when he visited the tiny Brigflatts Meeting House. The result was one of the major Modernist autobiographical poems – although spelt differently: *Briggflatts* (1966).

Charles Causley (1917–2003) Although he is widely revered for his writings about Cornwall, he trained as a teacher in Peterborough, the setting of the poem included here – one of his earliest ballads, a form he loved. 'Party' is naval slang for a girl, but the reference to Katharine of Aragon is misleading: she became Queen in her 20s but lived until she was 50, dying at Kimbolton Castle. Causley taught most of his life in Launceston, and might have appreciated the fact that in 1986 pupils from Kimbolton School marked the 450th anniversary of her death by carrying a mock coffin from the castle to the cathedral. Causley's poetry is a reminder that there are many kinds of localised Englishness.

Glen Cavaliero (1927–2019) A Cambridge don, a long-standing interest in English rural tradition is evident from his poetry (once highly acclaimed, but somewhat neglected) and critical writings. The 'Barnaby' mentioned in 'Going Places' is presumably DCI Barnaby from the television series, *Midsomer Murders.*

John Challis (1984–) His remarkable debut collection made much of his father's job as a taxi driver – 'The Knowledge' is the term used for the rigorous test of roads and routes that London cabbies have to undergo (currently under review to make it less demanding). The poem might be read as an urban version of Heaney's 'Digging'. Challis has a PhD in Creative Writing from Newcastle University and lives in Whitley Bay.

Richard Church (1893–1972) This Kentish celebrant of a somewhat mystical Englishness is largely remembered for his three volumes of autobiography. He was also married three times and had three daughters and a son. His beautifully honed verse has almost entirely dropped from view.

Kate Clanchy (1965–) Scottish by birth, she has lived in London's East End and Oxford. As in her poem here (about Cambridge), she is often inclined to challenge the status quo. Her poetry also tends to emphasise female experience.

David Clarke (1972–) Born in Lincolnshire, he has published two collections with Nine Arches, the most recent of which – *The Europeans* (2019) – is much concerned with what it means to be English during the era of Brexit.

David Constantine (1944–) From Salford, he lives in Oxford, where he is Fellow of the Queen's College, and in the Scilly Isles. Despite (or because of) his reputation as a translator of German poets, he is much concerned with Englishness in poetry and prose. His story 'Tea at the Midland' became the film *45 Years*, starring Tom Courtney and Charlotte Rampling.

Wendy Cope (1945–) From Kent, she studied at Oxford and became a primary-school teacher before her extraordinary success (with her Faber debut) in reviving those very English arts: parody and satire. She now lives in the Fens. In the days before dating apps, there was the Lonely Hearts column: an ingenious villanelle by Cope catches the clipped style of these newspaper ads. Love's technology has advanced, but the gist is much the same online or off.

Frances Cornford (1886–1960) Darwin was her grandfather, the poet John Cornford was her son and Cambridge was the centre of her world (the 'Backs' are the attractive grounds behind the colleges). She struggled to be taken seriously by the influential anthologist Edward Marsh, despite recommendations from Rupert Brooke.

Fred D'Aguiar (1960–) Born in London, he spent his early years in Guyana, and the Caribbean is a constant presence in his poetry, which has been very influential. He has also written novels and plays.

Peter Daniels (1954–) He is author of several witty poetry collections and a translator of Vladislav Khodasevich. He has been a Hawthornden Fellow and Queer Writer in Residence at the London Metropolitan Archives. Born in Cambridge, he grew up in Birmingham and now lives in Stoke Newington. Ironically, his poem 'Being English' is in that most exotic form, the ghazal.

Elizabeth Daryush (1887–1977) The daughter of Robert Bridges, she grew up in Oxford. She had an abiding interest in English flora, fostered by her father, which is evident in her poetry. She married a Persian and lived in Persia (Iran) before returning to Boar's Hill near Oxford in the 1920s.

Rishi Dastidar (1977–) A Londoner (as the title of his poem here would suggest), he pinpoints his love of poetry to an occasion in a now-vanished Oxford Street bookshop when he picked up Michael Hofmann's translations of Durs Grünbein. He has three collections from Nine Arches, and he has had poems in the *Financial Times*, *New Scientist* and on the BBC.

C. Day Lewis (1904–72) Anglo-Irish, one of the Thirties Poets, active as a communist before settling into the establishment and the Laureateship. He is even buried next to Hardy in Stinsford, Dorset. The poem included here is the 32nd section of his sequence 'The Magnetic Mountain', which was published by the

Hogarth Press in their second Living Poets series and dedicated to Auden. The name Day Lewis is probably better known these days through the work of his actor son, Daniel.

Imtiaz Dharker (1954–) Pakistani-born, a film maker, artist and prolific poet based in London, she is well known to GCSE students – as well as to the late Queen, since she received her Gold Medal for Poetry and turned down the chance to be Laureate in 2019 – and is one of the few serious poets to have been invited on to *Desert Island Discs.*

Patric Dickinson (1914–94) Born in India, he excelled at many things, including golf. He was a Professor of Rhetoric, a producer at the BBC, wrote plays, biographies, translations (from Greek and Latin). During World War II he served in the Artists' Rifles (like Edward Thomas).

Jane Draycott (1954–) A Londoner, she likes to explore mysterious aspects of landscape and social history, combining the lucid, the playful and the dreamlike. She has translated the medieval 'dream poem', *Pearl*, which seems to be one of the influences (is Ishiguro another?) on the title poem we have chosen from her 2022 collection, *The Kingdom*. Our other choice, 'The Road', centres on Wayland's Smithy, a Neolithic long barrow in Oxfordshire.

Carol Ann Duffy (1955–) She was born in Glasgow and in recent years has been Professor and Director of the Creative Writing School in Manchester. Her plays are as popular as her poems. Both have explored dark areas, but during her spell as Laureate some brighter rays broke through to illuminate aspects of Englishness. Here she boldly ventures on to the White Cliffs of Dover, fearless of cliché (or Vera Lynn), and untypically allusive: Matthew Arnold's 'Dover Beach' and Shakespeare's *King Lear* are both in her mind.

T.S. Eliot (1888–1965) His family came from East Coker in Somerset, but he was born in Missouri. In spite of which, *Four Quartets* is perhaps the most English poem of the twentieth century, with three out of the four locations set in rural England. In *The Waste Land*, from much earlier, Eliot's sense of Englishness is largely urban and centred on London, but it reaches back through time – as in the Edmund Spenser quoted in our excerpt.

Steve Ely (1965–) Director of the Ted Hughes Network, he shares with Hughes a fascination with landscape and wildlife (birds and – perhaps led by his surname – eels), along with a passion for the mythology in everyday Englishness – or Yorkshireness.

Gavin Ewart (1916–95) Remembered for some scurrilous light verse and a few genuinely moving poems, he was born in London. He attended Wellington School and the same Cambridge college as Milton. One wonders what the puritanical Lady of Christ's would have made of Ewart. Indeed, what did Grantham-born Mrs Thatcher make of the last lines of his Christmas poem, in the unlikely event that she had time to read them in 1982?

U.A. Fanthorpe (1929–2009) She taught at Cheltenham Ladies College before becoming 'a middle-aged dropout' and working as a hospital receptionist while she wrote. Her poems seemed to fill the gap left by the death of Betjeman, exploring both light and dark aspects of Englishness – and of the English language.

Elaine Feinstein (1930–2019) Poet, biographer, translator, playwright, memoirist Elaine Feinstein was from Bootle, Lancashire but grew up in Leicester. Both London and Cambridge (she was at Newnham) became important to her and her poetry. She was a writer of international scope, whose Jewishness was central to her work. Her poem 'England' alludes to a scene in *Antony and Cleopatra* when 'music i' th'air' suggests that Hercules has finally lost patience and is perhaps turning to the more youthful hero, Octavius (later Octavian, then Augustus). It is a moment also captured by Cavafy in 'The God Abandons Antony'.

Matthew Francis (1956–) He is from Winchester and originally worked in the computer industry, but after several Faber collections is now Professor of Creative Writing at Aberystwyth. Although often drawn to Welsh culture, he has an abiding fascination with Englishness and, in the poem here, English place names.

John Gohorry (1943–2021) Always something of an outsider, perhaps because his books could be rather strange or simply very long and intimidating, nevertheless he was a remarkable poet – one for ever associated with Letchworth Garden City. He is fitly commemorated in Stuart Henson's 2022 Festschrift, *Bold Heart*. Costa Brava has been from the very earliest days of the package holiday one of the most popular cheap destinations for the generally monoglot English.

Lorna Goodison (1947–) She was born and grew up in Jamaica, and began as a painter before specialising in poetry. She has taught and performed around the world, and is currently a professor in Michigan. She received the 2019 Queen's Gold Medal for Poetry.

John Greening (1954–) Although he is undoubtedly British, he recognises much that is precious to him in the word 'English': it is involved with his love of walking, music and, of course, poetry. His new Selected Poems, *The Interpretation of Owls* (2023), edited by Kevin Gardner is, ironically enough, published in America.

Geoffrey Grigson (1905–85) John Greening's 2017 Selected edition was an attempt to revive some interest in this once very well-known poet and much feared critic, who lived in (and dearly loved) Wiltshire. But it was Grigson's writings about the English countryside and his classic *The Englishman's Flora* (1955) that made his name. The 'Heath' in his poem here would be Hampstead Heath. 'Searchlights and Bombers' (originally 'The Bombers') resembles Stevie Smith's poem in making something sexual of the bombing raids.

Philip Gross (1952–) Astonishingly prolific and versatile, he was born in Delabole, Cornwall, near a slate quarry, which was once the largest man-made hole in Europe. His father was an Estonian refugee and Gross is fascinated by identity, but even more by English ritual and myth. His Quaker beliefs are increasingly evident. The Stanley Spencer painting which prompted Gross's 'Apple Gatherers' dates from the artist's time at the Slade, and he considered it his 'first ambitious work'. It can be viewed on Tate Britain's website. Gross's 'Between the Islands' is set in Somerset; a 'rhyne' is a drainage ditch.

Thom Gunn (1929–2004) Born in Gravesend, he spent much of his life in the gay community on America's West Coast, though there are several London poems. Influenced by Elizabethan and Jacobean poets (Fulke Greville, Ben Jonson), even his most free-and-easy American poems betray a certain Anglo-Saxon reticence, a formal, quasi-metaphysical Englishness.

Ivor Gurney (1890–1937) This troubled Gloucestershire composer and poet is only now emerging from the shadows of misprint and misunderstanding, with a revelatory new edition of his poetry in preparation. The one thing that brought him to life in the Dartford asylum was when Edward Thomas's widow brought him Ordnance Survey maps to pore over.

J.C. Hall (1920–2011) Born in Ealing, he grew up in Tunbridge Wells. Although a pacifist, he was nevertheless executor to war poet Keith Douglas. The poetry has been rather overlooked despite a 2003 selection from Shoestring Press.

Thomas Hardy (1840–1928) Hardy is not only associated with a recognisable area of England, he all but created it in his 'Wessex' novels. The poems inhabit the same Dorset landscape. The popular elegiac picture of a lost Englishness must be largely down to Hardy, who was an underrated poet before (and long after) he was a best-selling novelist. Some of the names in 'Voices from Things Growing...' may be found on graves in Stinsford churchyard.

Seamus Heaney (1939–2013) Heaney on Englishness? Unexpectedly, yes – responding to the troubles associated with the Reformation (and so connected to his own Troubles) he evokes the Fenland landscape around the cathedral city of Ely during stubble-burning, a familiar and stirring rite of the countryside, long since banned. By mentioning Will Brangwen, he also summons Nottinghamshire's own iconoclast, D.H. Lawrence.

Adrian Henri (1932–2000) If his high watermark as a poet was *The Mersey Sound* (Penguin Modern Poets 10, 1967), and although he never quite achieved the household status of Patten or McGough, he produced one of the era's most characteristic and convincing poems when he conjured the spirit of Blake (and the manner of Ginsberg) to address 'Mrs Albion'.

Stuart Henson (1954–) A Huntingdonshire poet – the story of 'Bridge' is true – who published firstly with Harry Chambers (in Cornwall), then with John Lucas (in Nottingham), both bastions of Englishness. Stuart taught for many years in Kimbolton and has written and produced several plays, including adaptations of Ian Serraillier and John Steinbeck.

Geoffrey Hill (1932–2016) Worcestershire, specifically Bromsgrove, was his home ground (his father was a policeman) and the prose poems of his *Mercian Hymns* (1971) are the glorious fruit of that childhood. His subsequent work could be tough and bitter, too lofty to reach, but on the common ground of the English countryside he was unrivalled.

Michael Hofmann (1957–) Born in Freiburg, Germany, he has become one of the most sophisticated chroniclers of Englishness as the poem included here suggests. As a distinguished translator, he knows how to capture what is idiomatic and to recreate it in another form. It is often the 'outsider' who sees things as they are.

Molly Holden (1927–81) Born in Peckham, she settled in Wiltshire and found a following just as she herself was in decline with multiple sclerosis; but her poems – Hardyesque, with a touch of Housman – are some of the finest nature poems of the period.

Holly Hopkins Born and brought up in Berkshire, then London, she now lives in Manchester. She has received an Eric Gregory Award for poets under thirty and a Hawthornden Fellowship. *The English Summer* (2022) is her first full collection.

A.E. Housman (1859–1936) Born in Fockbury, educated in Bromsgrove, Housman worked for a decade at the Patent Office, but was elected a Fellow of Trinity College, Cambridge in 1911. *A Shropshire Lad* (1896) was the collection most likely to be found in a World War I soldier's knapsack and still helps shape our idea of Englishness. His repressed homosexuality has been the subject of much scrutiny and more than one play.

Sarah Howe (1983–) Born in Hong Kong to an English father and a Chinese mother, Sarah Howe made that the focus of her debut, *Loop of Jade*, which won the T.S. Eliot Prize in 2016. She teaches at King's College, London and is a scholar of Renaissance English poetry (she has a poem about the Countess of Pembroke's Arcadia).

Glyn Hughes (1935–2011) Born in Altrincham, he was devoted to Yorkshire and his own patch at Mill Bank, near Sowerby Bridge. A respected novelist, his poems are often very fine and sometimes the equal of the Other Hughes. The John Taverner at the end of his poem is the fifteenth–sixteenth-century composer, and the Boston he mentions is the one in Lincolnshire.

Ted Hughes (1930–98) From his early 'Pike' in a pond 'as deep as England' to the landscapes of *Moortown*, *Season Songs* and *Remains of Elmet*, he was a man for whom a Yorkshire-inflected (or Devonshire-crusted) Englishness was the stuff of life. He was also a fisherman and, as 'Last Load' suggests, a farmer. His Moortown 'diary' poems, which he hardly considered poems himself, are among his best work. This poem was dated 20 June 1975.

Elizabeth Jennings (1926–2001) One of the few women poets of the 50s 'Movement', she had a considerable following for her intensely spiritual poems, in which there was an aura of England, though an even headier scent of Rome. She usually declines to identify places, but 'Somerset' here is an exception.

Brian Jones (1938–2009) Born in Islington, educated at Cambridge, he worked mainly in Kent. A very welcome *New & Selected Poems* (2013) reminded readers of why he was once widely praised. Sadly, he was always less well known than a certain Rolling Stone. He is a poet of Englishness and English history par excellence.

Sidney Keyes (1922–43) A poet with a broad international outlook from the start, he was astonishingly precocious at Oxford. Born in Dartford the same year Ivor Gurney was incarcerated there, he regretted not coming from Oxfordshire or Wiltshire, wishing he were a pastoral poet like Edward Thomas. Like Thomas, he died fighting in a world war – in Tunisia.

Mimi Khalvati (1944–) Born in Tehran, she was brought up on the Isle of Wight, which features in some important early poems; in later work there is more of London, where she lives. There is much formal variety, the ghazal and the sonnet being favourites. She was an actor before turning to poetry.

Zaffar Kunial Born in Birmingham to an English mother and a Kashmiri father, he lives in Yorkshire. His poetry engages vigorously with the English tradition (his Polesworth, for instance, is associated with Drayton and Donne), and his latest Faber collection alludes to Blake in its title: *England's Green*.

Philip Larkin (1922–85) He was born in Coventry ('Nothing, like something, happens anywhere'), but is more readily associated with Hull – his departure point in 'The Whitsun Weddings', a poem driven by undercurrents of symbolism. Larkin believed he had escaped the influence of Yeats, but both W.B. and Blake would have appreciated that arrow shower.

D.H. Lawrence (1885–1930) Nottinghamshire was the now somewhat unfashionable novelist and poet's *fons et origo*. Even though he often lived abroad he could not resist pawing at Englishness. The satirical rhymes here may surprise those who know only the free-verse animal poems and rather doubt his sense of humour. They refer to the fact that his paintings were seized by Scotland Yard when they went on display in 1929 soon after the publication of *Lady Chatterley's Lover*.

Gregory Leadbetter (1975–) He studied at Cambridge but gave up a law career to focus on writing. He has written for the BBC and published widely on the Romantics. He is now Professor of Poetry at Birmingham City, with two collections out from Nine Arches. The nature of Englishness is one of the many concerns in his powerful and original poetry. Up until Tudor times in England (although the custom may originate with Roman Saturnalia) a Lord of Misrule would be chosen by lot to preside over the Christmas festivities.

Denise Levertov (1923–97) This important American poet grew up in Ilford, Essex (she was home-schooled) and her poems regularly glance back to England. Her political concerns and indignations were always fiery, but there is a profound spiritual note in her later work. Significantly, Samuel Palmer's blossoming tree adorns the jacket of her 2013 *Collected*. Perhaps she is thinking of the Stewartby brickworks, but also of Bunyan when she guesses at Bedfordshire in her poem about a train journey, although the phrase 'earthly paradise' is from William Morris.

Grevel Lindop (1948–) A versatile poet from Liverpool, he was Professor of Romantic and Early Victorian Studies at Manchester University. He has written books on de Quincey and Charles Williams, a guide to the Lakes and a series of poems about strip clubs. He is closely associated with Kathleen Raine's Temenos Academy. Silbury, mentioned in his poem, is a mysterious prehistoric chalk mound near Avebury in Wiltshire.

Edward Lowbury (1913–2007) An eminent microbiologist by profession, he was based in Birmingham. Growing up in London, he mixed with friends of Yeats such as Sturge Moore. He is one of the few English-language poets who can say (to John Greening's eternal envy) that Sibelius admired his verse, but the poem here is about that merriest, most eccentrically English of musicians, Imogen Holst.

Hannah Lowe (1976–) When in 2021 the winner of the last ever Costa Prize was announced to be a relatively unknown poet, there was much excitement. The winner, *The Kids*, is a series of sonnets about an inner-city school. Lowe has a Jamaican-Chinese father (the subject of an earlier book), and she clearly empathises with the immigrant students.

Louis MacNeice (1907–63) He was born in Belfast, but went to school in Marlborough, lectured on classics in Birmingham and became a features producer for the BBC in London. All three locations turn up in his poems. He is one of a number of Irish poets able to capture an indefinable something about the English landscape and character. His extraordinary long poem, 'Autumn Journal', captures the pre-war mood: our excerpt is from Section VIII, the time of Chamberlain's flight to Munich to negotiate with Hitler.

Jack Mapanje (1944–) A Malawian writer, he was imprisoned from 1987–91 for his poetry collection *Chameleons and Gods*, which dared to criticise the Government. It was during his time in London that he wrote the poem included here, with its complex feelings about English liberties.

Glyn Maxwell (1962–) Generally associated with Welwyn Garden City, he is a poet of immense scope who studied with Derek Walcott. Despite the effervescent quality (he is an actor and playwright), there is a meditative streak, which comes out in his Edward Thomas sequence. The 'Video Tale of a Patriot' is more characteristic of its decade – a virtuoso performance piece well suited to the actor-poet.

Charlotte Mew (1869–1928) At last Mew is receiving her due with a new Faber Selected. Often compared to Hardy (who admired her), she spent virtually her entire life in Bloomsbury. Her country monologues are products of imagination, yet 'The Trees are Down' is a kind of pastoral. Mew was a somewhat liberated woman, doing as she pleased (she rolled her own cigarettes), despite poor mental health.

Kei Miller (1970–) A Jamaican poet, he came to England to study Creative Writing in Manchester and now divides his time between the two countries. Consequently, he is perceptive about the racial tensions and cultural fault lines that run through English society, and his poetry deals with such issues in a witty, sophisticated style. The 'dasheen' he mentions is a starchy vegetable well known in Jamaica.

Dom Moraes (1938–2004) This Mumbai poet won the Hawthornden Prize while still at Oxford, and received considerable attention when he became one of the Penguin Modern Poets with Kingsley Amis and Peter Porter. He is better known in India these days.

Andrew Motion (1952–) A former Poet Laureate, he was responsible for reclaiming Englishness as a respectable theme with his early poems, which even touched on tricky colonial issues. More persistently, he has written elegies for his mother (and here for his father too) set in pastoral landscapes. There is a direct line from Blunden to Motion.

Daljit Nagra (1966–) Born in West Drayton near Heathrow, he grew up in Sheffield and broke on to the scene with his allusively titled first collection for Faber: *Look We Have Coming to Dover!* (2007). More recently came *British Museum* (2017). His exploration of the innards and interstices of English behaviour has been refreshing and challenging.

Katrina Naomi From Margate (whose sands were immortalised by Eliot), she was 'brought up working class' and confesses to having been 'expelled from school', like a surprising number of distinguished writers. She has since been welcomed to Cornwall, where she is astonishingly active as a poet. Her last two books are from Seren, and she won the 2021 Keats-Shelley Prize.

Grace Nichols (1950–) She left Guyana for the UK in 1977, and seems to find a certain electricity in connecting the two locations, as in her piece, a popular exam text, 'Hurricane Hits England' and more subtly in the poem included here. Her later work seems calmer, frequently funny, increasingly interested in Englishness (she has a poem about the 'leisurely conviviality' of tea).

Norman Nicholson (1914–87) Once considered a major poet, prominent on Faber's list, he is now very much a provincial figure, whose subject matter rarely ranges beyond Cumbria; yet few modern poets evoke the Lake District as wonderfully. He never moved from the small house in Millom where he grew up, and where he was bedbound because of TB, as described here. There are currently efforts to preserve his home for the nation.

Sean O'Brien (1952–) He grew up in Hull and lives in Newcastle upon Tyne, and his work is alive with the spirit of northern England, including its painful memories. There is a strong political and mischievous edge to the (very formal) verse, tempered by his almost Kiplingesque gift for elegy.

Dennis O'Driscoll (1954–2012) Best known as the interviewer in *Stepping Stones*, Heaney's 'autobiography', O'Driscoll was a very popular poet in Ireland after the success of his satire, 'The Bottom Line'. He loved England and certain English poets (e.g. Michael Hamburger), and his long poem here makes a refreshing change from all the English commentary on Ireland, and largely resists irony. NB. The editors have decided to retain O'Driscoll's somewhat inconsistent use of italics and inverted commas.

Ruth Padel (1946–) This prolific, wide-ranging and fiercely intelligent poet was born in Wimpole Street and is the great-great grandchild of Darwin, whom she has honoured with a book-length poem. The earlier poem included here demonstrates her love of historical narrative and the shades of expression it offers (and a very Darwinian knowledge of plants).

Fiona Pitt-Kethley (1954–) An unexpectedly sexy brand of poetry emerged with Pitt-Kethley's first books in the 1980s: they belong to an English tradition that stretches back at least as far as Aphra Behn. She was born in Edgware and lived for many years in Hastings.

Sylvia Plath (1932–63) One of the countless original elements to Plath's poetry is the way she brings a personal and New World perspective to Old World pastoral ('Wuthering Heights', 'Parliament Hill Fields') and rural traditions. The elm in her poem of that title here is undoubtedly an English Elm. The earlier poem about Grantchester – famously evoked by Rupert Brooke and for a while the home of Plath's biographer, Anne Stevenson – harks back to her days with Ted Hughes at Cambridge.

William Plomer (1903–73) A South African poet (unlike his English parents, he pronounced his name 'ploomer' – a more than English touch of exceptionalism), he became part of the literary establishment when he arrived in London from Japan, even writing a libretto for Britten.

Peter Porter (1929–2010) He was Australian, but became one of the most influential poetry and cultural critics in London – particularly astute on music. Unlike Les Murray or Judith Wright, he seldom wrote about his homeland, but the English tradition was grist to his hard-working, very un-Schubertian, poetic mill.

Neil Powell (1948–) Having been a teacher and a bookseller, he took to biography and produced fine lives of Roy Fuller, Kingsley and Martin Amis, George Crabbe and Benjamin Britten – often attracted by Suffolk connections. 'The Vanished Places' captures his adopted county's vulnerability to the sea. His quiet pastoral style emerged from the Movement, but Powell's sense of a literary tradition adds a special gravitas.

Frederic Prokosch (1906–89) Born in Wisconsin, his father a professor of linguistics, his mother a concert pianist, he was educated at Haverford, then Cambridge and Yale, and is remembered chiefly for his novels. During World War II he was a cultural attaché in Sweden, and the poem here, one of eleven wartime 'Landscapes', suggests he travelled widely – though English tea-making clearly eluded him. The descriptions of Pope and the Frenchman's words are also puzzling. He was (uniquely among poets?) a champion squash player.

Kathleen Raine (1908–2003) An authority on Blake and Yeats and indeed Samuel Palmer, she was a Londoner but grew up in Northumberland (the autobiographies are engrossing). She was one of the few women poets to rival the pack of Thirties men. Much of her work is mystically abstract, but her landscapes can be breathtaking, although one is grateful for the human touches.

James Reeves (1909–78) Born in Middlesex, he was educated at Stowe and Cambridge. He was initially a teacher, and achieved popularity for his children's writings. A champion of traditional English verse, he edited and anthologised prolifically. He was closely associated with Robert Graves.

Christopher Reid (1949–) Born in Hong Kong, he was educated in England. He was associated with the so-called Martian poets, but has outgrown them. His verse comedy 'A Song of Lunch' (adapted for television and stage) is one of his finest achievements; another is the elegy for his wife, 'A Scattering'. Reid gives voice to a more eccentric, unpredictable English quality which poets have tended to overlook.

Anne Ridler (1912–2001) She was born in Rugby to a family of teachers and writers. Overshadowed by T.S. Eliot, whose style she tended to imitate, she did manage to carve out something of a reputation, writing an important study of Charles Williams and seeing her verse dramas performed.

Roger Robinson (1967–) He lives between Brixton and Trinidad, and is an experienced performer who has toured internationally (notably for the British Council) and whose widely commissioned poems have won several awards. He was selected by Decibel as one of the 50 most influential Black writers. His collection *A Portable Paradise* – which focuses on the Grenfell Tower fire – won the 2019 T.S. Eliot Prize.

Carol Rumens (1944–) Born in south London, she has travelled widely, bringing a personal and political angle to her observations. Her *Guardian* 'Poem of the Week' blog has a considerable following. Hers is essentially a European voice, which she frequently uses to comment on England and Englishness. Her translations are rightly admired. The witty sestina included here is typical of her formal ingenuity.

Vita Sackville-West (1892–1962) The ancient seat of the Sackvilles at Knole is where she grew up, and the garden at Sissinghurst is the place most associated with her. Her life story is complicated, but it involves a relationship with Virginia Woolf and marriage to Harold Nicolson. Her best-known poetry collection is *The Land* (1926).

Siegfried Sassoon (1886–1967) The war poet's immensely wealthy family lived at Weirleigh in Kent, but he made his home at Heytesbury House in Wiltshire. A keen huntsman and cricket lover, he became a nationally known figure, whose poems Churchill claimed to know by heart – despite the trouble Sassoon's anti-war protests had caused. He is buried at Mells in Somerset near his friend, the priest and scholar Ronald Knox.

Tom Sastry (1974–) He grew up in Buckinghamshire and describes himself as a 'second-generation Original' since his mother is 'Originally English' and his father 'Originally Indian'.

His two recent collections give a highly entertaining new spin to some of the ideas in this anthology.

William Scammell (1939–2000) From a working-class family in Hythe, he lived for years in the Lake District (where 'English Zen' is set) and edited an anthology of New Lake Poets. He also produced a study of Keith Douglas and edited Ted Hughes's prose. A brilliant satirist, parodist and fearless critic, he could praise heartily when required. The poetry is irresistible and has been overlooked for too long.

E.J. Scovell (1907–99) Born in Eccleshall Bierlow near Sheffield the same year as Auden and MacNeice, she began publishing in the 40s and favoured something apolitical and altogether more reflective – although she was not religious, despite being the daughter of the village rector. There is, however, a peaceful, even mystical centre to her poems, whose Englishness is undeniable. She lived much of her life in Oxford.

Peter Scupham (1933–2022) If there is a tradition of Englishness, then Peter Scupham's immaculate and scrupulously formal work lies near its heart. 'Ploughland' presents a kind of pastoral stasis which Blunden would have recognised. Scupham was born in Bootle, taught in Letchworth for many years, and ran a successful small press (the Mandeville) as well as a second-hand book business, but later made a new life in an extraordinary manor house in rural Norfolk – renowned for its annual Poetry Picnic. He died while this anthology was in preparation.

Robert Selby (1984–) One of a new generation of poets unafraid to explore the idea of Englishness, often through its rural traditions, in a way that Edmund Blunden would have appreciated. He is especially attuned to that poet's native county, and his richly textured 2022 collection is titled *The Kentish Rebellion*.

Elisabeth Sennitt Clough (1974–) A poet of the Fens (she was born in Ely), she is anything but provincial. Her time in Fresno, California, has enabled her to look at English landscapes and manners through a Claude glass borrowed from the Beats. Her latest book, *My Name is Abilene*, is published by Salt and has been shortlisted for the Forward Prize Best Collection, 2023.

Jo Shapcott (1953–) A highly regarded and uncategorisable Faber poet who – in between her probing lyrics, personal elegies and surreal experiments – has occasionally dipped into the nature of Englishness. She is a Londoner and teaches at Royal Holloway. 'Phrase Book' is set during the Gulf War and uses military jargon of the time.

Penelope Shuttle (1947–) Like Peter Redgrove, with whom she will always be associated (hence her widely acclaimed collection, *Redgrove's Wife*, 2006), Shuttle delights in a place's mythical undercurrents – literally so in the case of her recent *Lyonesse* (2021). Her home has long been in Falmouth, but London fascinates her. In 2016 she and John Greening collaborated on *Heath*, poems about the area surrounding Heathrow. In 'Self-Portrait as Katharine of Aragon' she imagines herself as Henry VIII's Spanish Queen, separated from him and constantly shifting between prisons.

John Siddique (1964–) After a rebellious youth, he attended Manchester University and subsequently became a 'spiritual teacher' and poet who counts D.H. Lawrence (and the local library) among his influences. He has produced work for children as well as adults. He was Royal Literary Fund Writing Fellow in York.

Jon Silkin (1930–97) He was born in London, where he founded the influential magazine *Stand*, which he took with him (after some years working as a labourer) to Leeds, then Newcastle. He could be found selling it in pubs and cinema queues; it is still going strong. His writings about England always consider the underprivileged, the outsiders (his Jewishness is crucial here) and there is usually a political subtext. 'Strike' is from the sequence 'Killhope Wheel', set in County Durham.

C.H. Sisson (1914–2003) A Bristolian who retired to – and often wrote about – Somerset, he was once considered the foremost English poet, although as a right-wing senior civil servant he was an unlikely candidate, and tastes change. Yet the poetry remains potent, often angry yet winningly mysterious. His vast intellect and the range of his translations feed into even the simplest lyrics. Here is Englishness laid bare, or at least with only a metrical fig leaf.

Edith Sitwell (1887–1964) If *Façade* 1922) is her best-known work, then that is not untypical: it represents a certain kind of English eccentricity (she recited the poems to Walton's music using a megaphone through a decorated screen). But there are poems that go much deeper, such as the one included here about the Blitz. In it, she quotes lines from Marlowe's *Dr Faustus*. A recording of Sitwell reading the poem can be heard on The Poetry Archive.

Stevie Smith (1902–71) She was genuinely popular when there were few women poets being published, and she remains impossible to pin down. Much of her work bubbles childishly or flails around pointlessly, but then something makes startling contact with a truth. Palmers Green in London was the centre of her world. It's hard to imagine her as anything other than English.

Wole Soyinka (1934–) The Nobel Prize-winning Nigerian is known for his verse dramas, but also for one much-anthologised poem, which the current editors could not resist choosing yet again. But is it definitely set in England? The red bus, pillar-box and phone booth of 'Telephone Conversation', plus the 'Button A, Button B' technology give it away.

Muriel Spark (1918–2006) Google defines the Edinburgh born writer as a novelist only (and most people only know *The Prime of Miss Jean Brodie*), but in 2015 Carcanet brought out a selection of her poetry which had never been gathered before. It contains some gems. Spark lived in a bedsit in Camberwell before settling in Italy, but her poems visit various locations. Shipton-under-Wychwood, as described in her poem, is in Oxfordshire. Henry VII built a hunting lodge there, its now-shrunken forest particularly popular with the Tudors.

Stephen Spender (1909–95) A prominent writer of the Thirties group, he was eventually more celebrated for his gossipy journals than his verse, yet the landmark pieces are still strong – including 'The Pylons', whose lines carry as much power today as they did ninety years ago. The metal structures were no less controversial than the wind turbines of the twenty-first century.

John Squire (1884–1958) Plymouth-born, he became an influential editor and critic of Modernism, gathering around him his 'Squirearchy' (the Sitwells' quip). His poem about George V's Silver Jubilee has his usual easy-going, patriotic charm, and is a reminder that there were more voices in the 1930s than the so-called Thirties Poets – although J.C. Squire's ballad metre is worthy of any 'Macspaunday'.

Jon Stallworthy (1935–2014) He was an authority on Wilfred Owen and the World War I poets, and his sense of Englishness is inseparable from that. It's not surprising, then, that he reacted as he did to the Vietnam protest poems by non-combatants at the Royal Albert Hall, but his response caused quite a furore.

Margaret Stanley-Wrench (1916–74) One of the least familiar names in our anthology, this London-based poet was the daughter of a novelist and cookery writer, and became a friend of

Keith Douglas at Oxford. She had more success with children's books than with her poetry. Her poem is about Gilbert White (1720–93), the celebrated diarist and naturalist of Selborne, Hampshire. The Hangar (or 'Selborne Hanger', as it is usually termed and more properly spelt) is a steeply wooded hill just east of the village.

Anne Stevenson (1933–2020) American, yet devoted to Britain's people, poetry and landscape, especially the areas around Cambridge (she lived in Grantchester for a time) and Durham, where she finally settled. Her many collections, not to mention her no-nonsense criticism and the Plath biography, *Bitter Fame* (1989), won her much acclaim. She lived in and wrote about Wales and Scotland too, but few poets have captured England so exhilaratingly.

George Szirtes (1948) He was brought to the UK from Hungary during the revolution, and has made himself a pillar of English poetry (based in Norfolk). A master of metrical ingenuity, his artist's eye picks out details of English landscape and character that others might miss. 'What oft was thought but ne'er so well expressed'. In 'Scene at a Conference', the WVS is the Women's Voluntary Service, a World War II organisation.

Edward Thomas (1878–1917) If this war poet of depopulated landscapes, abandoned farmyards and inviting footpaths is the presiding genius of our anthology, it is because of an authenticity in his verse, a way of writing that follows rules while gently breaking them. He had absorbed much of the best writing about Englishness before he gave up his literary career and enlisted. When Eleanor Farjeon asked what he was fighting for, he famously picked up 'a pinch of earth' and said, 'Literally, for this.'

Anthony Thwaite (1930–2021) He was influential long before his work on Larkin, editing important anthologies and (that rare thing) a TV series about English poetry. Born in Chester, he worked as a radio producer at the BBC in London – for a while with MacNeice – then moved to Norfolk with his biographer wife, Ann. His love of poetry apparently began when he tried writing Anglo-Saxon riddles at school.

Charles Tomlinson (1927–2015) Perhaps more celebrated abroad than at home, and much influenced by Americans such as William Carlos Williams, nevertheless he became the most English of poets. His later work frequently evokes Gloucestershire landscapes, but it was his native Stoke-on-Trent that first showed him 'The Way In' – the title, in fact, of the collection from which 'Gladstone Street' is chosen.

Rosemary Tonks (1928–2014) She vanished from the literary scene in the 70s after two exceptionally fine collections. Her vision of English city life ('Bedouin of the London Evening') owes much to French symbolists. An annotated Collected edited by Neil Astley came out in the year of her death, and has restored her to the canon.

John Wain (1925–94) It says much for his reputation that this poet and novelist didn't change his name, but in fact Wain became Oxford Professor of Poetry, and his lectures are some of his finest work. The verse is little read today, yet the example here suggests it is time for a revival.

Derek Walcott (1930–2017) We associate the Nobel Laureate with St Lucia, but he wrote a good deal about Britain, sometimes critically, but also with affectionate nostalgia. His splendid book-length poem about Pissarro is one example, but there are other glances at Englishness. The lines here summon the mood of a Gloucestershire orchard out of *Henry IV, Part 2*. Walcott, like Shakespeare, was a verse dramatist.

Sylvia Townsend Warner (1893–1978) Her novels are much admired, but surely it is the poetry which is her chief claim to fame beyond Dorset – where she and Valentine Ackland are rightly commemorated in the Dorchester museum. She is inclined to the pastoral, yet she is never superficial or sentimental about England. There is a complex musicality to her work, a reminder that she was herself a musician who helped prepare the ten volumes of *Tudor Music* for OUP.

Rory Waterman (1981–) He was born in Belfast (the son of the poet Andrew Waterman) and lives in Nottingham, where he teaches Creative Writing, but Lincolnshire is especially important to him. He grew up on the edge of a country estate in Nocton (one of his poems just has a map reference for title). His verse provides some of the sharpest and most enjoyable commentary on what it now means to be English and/or British. The date of 'Driving through the Pit Town' is significant, the poet has said, because it marks the death of Mrs Thatcher, who was much hated in the mining communities. Hence 'DING DONG!' (i.e. 'the witch is dead').

Rebecca Watts (1983–) She was born in Suffolk and studied at Cambridge, where she lives. She edited a fine edition of Elizabeth Jennings, with whom she has something in common. Her understated verse is already outliving noisier, flashier work, as typified by the very unWordsworthian daffodil poem here.

Kit Wright (1944–) One of our anthology's many poets born in Kent (perhaps because it's a county that rhymes so readily), he is based in London. Whether or not he is still Britain's tallest poet, Wright is one of the funniest, and not only in his children's poetry. He is certainly one of the most adept with often very complex rhyme and metre. It's hard to imagine who else would write a formal ode apostrophising Didcot Power Station – or the mock elegy on Wandsworth included here, which might be describing Camelot. Englishness and laughter are inseparable.

Note: Where no dates have been given it is at the request of the author.

INDEX OF TITLES

INDEX OF POETS

INDEX OF FIRST LINES

Great Britain impoverished to post-war prosperity, 81
Green slated gables clasp the stem of the hill, 204
Here they went with smock and crook, 49
I go on and on in England, 158
I have a queen's reason, 56
I have hardly set foot upon your soil, 211
I heard those voices today again, 227
I know the bottom, she says. I know it with my great tap root, 190
I saw her glide, lighter than air , 140
I think it's time it withered, let us go, 128
I walk through Brixton with a young man, 80
I was hungry, 58
I would hope for the children of West Ham, 268
I'm standing here inside my skin, 197
In this country, Jamaica is not quite as far, 35
In the old abbey chancel, in the apse, on the floor, 155
In this high pasturage, this Blunden time, 44
in your verdant years of nostalgia, cloud-harassed, 34
Into the silk blue sky it sails, 206
Is. Your. Mother. English? demands the Welsh girl, 64
It was my bridal night I remember, 210
It is a kingdom, a continent, 115
It was the place to go in nineteen-thirty, 164
January's grey and slushy, 129
King of the perennial holly-groves, the riven sandstone, 157
Land-islands, like their own astonishments, 59
Lovers on the Heath lie, and raise, 247
Lovers who would pet and fondle, 149
Midwinter spring is its own season, 217
Mist is your mother, Englishman, 221
Morning is a revealing; confession of rivers, 220
My dead father, who never knew what hit him, 91
My English grandfather, whose name in my father's language, 84
Next year we are to bring the soldiers home , 192
Not the knowledge chosen for the national, 52
Note nothing of why or how, enquire, 248
Now is the time for the burning of the leaves, 231
O silly little, proud and silly, country, 139
O you haunting ghosts, I move towards you, 130
Of a day's motoring, of half England left behind, 273
Oh what a pity, Oh! don't you agree, 262

ACKNOWLEDGEMENTS

The editors would like to express our deep gratitude to Will Dady and Renard Press; to Ian McMillan for his enthusiasm for this project, for understanding our aims, and for encapsulating them so well in his lovely foreword; to Baylor University for funding assistance; and to Lois Avey for her indefatigable assistance with our copyright fee payments.

For their generous contributions to our research, including advice in tracking down copyright holders and for graciously answering our research queries, we are grateful to Susanna Abse; Chris Aguirre, Penguin Random House USA; Bob Archambeau, Lake Forest College, Illinois; Neil Astley, Bloodaxe Books; M. Kwesi Brathwaite; Veronica Brusilovski, The Wylie Agency Ltd. USA; Stephen Claughton; Daniel DiLandro, Buffalo State University Archives; Lisa Dowdeswell, Society of Authors; Helen Fisher, Cadbury Research Library, University of Birmingham; Moira Fitzgerald and Jessica Tubis, Beinecke Rare Book and Manuscript Library, Yale University; Laura Forker, Penguin Random House UK; Victoria Fox, Farrar, Straus & Giroux; Jade Francis, Channing School, London; Elizabeth Garver, Harry Ransom Center, University of Texas; Douglas Greene, Old Dominion University, Virginia; Genny Grim, Pembroke College Library, Cambridge; Alexei Grinbaum, the Joseph Brodsky Estate; Paul Hartle, St Catharine's College, Cambridge; Lily Herd, *TLS*; Colin Higgins, St Catharine's College Library, Cambridge; Stuart Henson; Liz Jones-Minsinger, Haverford College Archives, Pennsylvania; Martin Killeen, Cadbury Research Library, University of Birmingham; Simon Knott;

Ellen Kurath; Gael Kurath; Philip Lancaster; Saffron Mackay, Royal College of Surgeons of England; Lorraine Mariner, National Poetry Library; James Maynard, The Poetry Collection, University at Buffalo; Steve Mielke, Harry Ransom Center, University of Texas; John Mole; Kate O'Donnell, Somerville College, Oxford; Rob Payne, Jesus College, Cambridge; Eric Prokosch; Martin Robson-Riley, The National Library of Wales; Katie Small, Lambeth Palace Library; Stephen Stuart-Smith, Enitharmon Press; David Sutton, WATCH File; Suzanna Tamminen, Wesleyan University Press; Jayne Taylor-Bain, The Charles Causley Trust; Peter Vertacnik; Claire Weatherall, Hull University Archives; Laura Whitaker-Jones; and Sarah-Jean Zubair.

For assistance with permissions, copyrights, and licensing fees, we are grateful to Susanna Abse; Chris Aguirre and Sherri Marmon, Penguin Random House USA; Simon Armitage; Pippa Barlow, The Wylie Agency Ltd. UK; Alan Brenik, Carcanet Press; Mary Brower and Peter London, HarperCollins; Nicola Carpenter and Gerard Holden; Kate Clanchy; Jane Commane and Peggy Long, Nine Arches Press; Tom Cornford; Rosangela da Cunha, Natalia Kourniokhova, and Carla Roda, PLSclear; Matt Dissen, Melanie Jackson Agency; Rosie Dunnett, Penned in the Margins; Jane Ewart; Suzanne Fairless-Aitken, Bloodaxe Books; Dan Fenton, Peters Fraser + Dunlop; Laura Forker, Lauren Bryson, and Jane Mowles, Penguin Random House UK; Victoria Fox, Farrar, Straus & Giroux; Tony Frazer, Shearsman Books; Georgia Glover, Sophia Rahim, and Tina Navin, David Higham Associates; Polly Halladay and Rachel Conway, Georgina Capel Associates; Duff Hart-Davis; Stuart Henson; Suella Holland, The Gallery Press; Liz Hughes; Olivia Kumar, RCW Literary Agency; Zaffar Kunial; Ellen Kurath; Ruth Lowbury; John Lucas, Shoestring Press; Olivia Martin and Seren Adams, United Agents; Lizzie Milne and Darren Barnes, C&W Agency; Ruth Padel; Eric Prokosch; Nicola Robert, St Catharine's College,

Cambridge; Jess Rollitt, Smith/Doorstop and Poetry Business; Vicki Salter, Barbara Levy Agency; Jan Scammell; Rob Selby; Elisabeth Sennitt-Clough; John Siddique; Lemn Sissay; Dan Smith; Karla Smith, Baylor University; Sarayu Srivatsa; Roger Squire; Stephen Stuart-Smith, Enitharmon Press; Becky Taylor, Faber and Faber; Rachel Taylor, David Godwin Associates; Rachel Thorne, Curtis Brown UK; Ann Thwaite; Ian Venables; Will Wain; Christopher Wait, New Directions Publishing; Elisabeth Wiedemann, Piper Verlag; Elizabeth Winkler, Curtis Brown USA; and Kit Wright.

CREDITS AND PERMISSIONS

The original publication source of each poem is provided here, followed by relevant copyright and reprint permission credits. The editors and publisher are grateful to the many copyright holders, publishers and representatives for their permission to reproduce copyrighted material. Every effort has been made to contact the copyright holders of the poems that comprise this collection; in the case of error or oversight, the copyright holder is encouraged to contact the publisher so that appropriate arrangements can be made. Works in the public domain are noted with *. Works whose copyrights we were unable to trace are noted with †.

Dannie Abse: 'Demo against the Vietnam War, 1968', *Funland and Other Poems* (Hutchinson, 1973). Reprinted by kind permission of Susanna Abse.

Valentine Ackland: 'Instructions from England, 1936', *Left Review* (March 1936); *Journey from Winter: Selected Poems*, ed. Frances Bingham (Carcanet, 2008). Reproduced by kind permission of Carcanet Press, Manchester, UK.

Gillian Allnutt: 'About Benwell', *Blackthorn* (Bloodaxe, 1994); *How the Bicycle Shone: New & Selected Poems* (Bloodaxe, 2007). Reproduced with permission of Bloodaxe Books. www.bloodaxe.com.

Moniza Alvi: 'Presents from My Aunts in Pakistan', *The Country at My Shoulder* (Oxford, 1993); *Split World: Poems 1990–2005* (Bloodaxe, 2008). Reproduced with permission of Bloodaxe Books. www.bloodaxe.com.

Raymond Antrobus: 'For Cousin John', *All the Names Given* (Picador, 2021). Reproduced by permission of David Higham Associates.

Simon Armitage: 'A Vision', *Tyrannosaurus Rex versus the Corduroy Kid* (Faber, 2006). Reproduced by permission of the author, of Faber and Faber Ltd., and of David Godwin Associates.

William Scammell: 'English Zen', *Black and White* (Flambard, 2002). Reprinted by kind permission of Jan Scammell and Ben Scammell.

E.J. Scovell: 'A Room at Nightfall', *Shadows of Chrysanthemums* (Routledge, 1944); *Collected Poems* (Carcanet, 1996). Reproduced by kind permission of Carcanet Press, Manchester, UK.

Peter Scupham: 'Ploughland', *Prehistories* (Oxford University Press, 1975); *Collected Poems* (Carcanet, 2002). Reproduced by kind permission of Carcanet Press, Manchester, UK.

Robert Selby: 'Chevening (X)', *The Coming-Down Time* (Shoestring, 2020). Reprinted by kind permission of John Lucas.

Elisabeth Sennitt Clough: 'Kerrie', *Sightings* (Pindrop Press, 2016). Reprinted by kind permission of the author.

Jo Shapcott: 'Phrase Book', *Phrase Book* (Oxford University Press, 1992). Reprinted by permission of the author and of Georgina Capel Associates Ltd.

Penelope Shuttle: 'Self-Portrait as Katharine of Aragon', *Father Lear* (Poetry Salzburg, 2020). Reprinted by kind permission of the author and of David Higham Associates.

John Siddique: 'A Map of Rochdale', *Poems from a Northern Soul* (Crocus, 2007). Reprinted by kind permission of the author.

Jon Silkin: 'Strike', *The Principle of Water* (Carcanet, 1974); *Complete Poems*, ed. Jon Glover and Kathryn Jenner (Carcanet, 2015). Reproduced by kind permission of Carcanet Press, Manchester, UK.

C.H. Sisson: 'Broadmead Brook', *What and Who* (Carcanet, 1994); *Collected Poems* (Carcanet, 1998). Reproduced by kind permission of Carcanet Press, Manchester, UK.

Edith Sitwell: 'Still Falls the Rain' *TLS* (6 September 1941); *Collected Poems* (Sinclair-Stevenson, 1993). 'Still Falls the Rain' from *Collected Poems* by Edith Sitwell reproduced by permission of Peters Fraser + Dunlop on behalf of the Estate of Edith Sitwell.

Stevie Smith: 'I Remember', *Not Waving but Drowning* (André Deutsch, 1957). Reproduced by permission of the Estate of Stevie Smith and of Faber and Faber Ltd. 'I Remember' by Stevie Smith, from *COLLECTED POEMS OF STEVIE SMITH*, copyright ©1972 by Stevie Smith. Reprinted by permission of New Directions Publishing Corp.

Wole Soyinka: 'Telephone Conversation', *Modern Poetry from Africa*, ed. Gerald Moore and Ulli Beier (Penguin, 1963). Reprinted by permission of the Melanie Jackson Agency.

Sylvia Townsend Warner: 'The Sad Shepherd', *Time Importuned* (Chatto & Windus, 1928); *New Collected Poems*, ed. Claire Harman (Carcanet, 2008). Reproduced by kind permission of Carcanet Press, Manchester, UK.

Rory Waterman: 'Driving through the Pit Town', *Sarajevo Roses* (Carcanet, 2017). Reproduced by kind permission of Carcanet Press, Manchester, UK.

Rebecca Watts: 'Daffodils push through in the mild first days of January', *Red Gloves* (Carcanet, 2020). Reproduced by kind permission of Carcanet Press, Manchester, UK.

Kit Wright: 'Wailing in Wandsworth', *Bump-Starting the Hearse* (Hutchinson, 1983). Reprinted by kind permission of the author.

Epigraphs

U.A. Fanthorpe: Extract from 'Found on the Battlefield', *Consequences* (Peterloo, 2000); *Selected Poems* (Enitharmon, 2013). Reprinted by kind permission of Dr R.V. Bailey and Stephen Stuart-Smith.

Stuart Henson: Extract from 'Nocturnall', *Ember Music* (Peterloo, 1994). Reprinted by kind permission of the author.

Ted Hughes: Extract from 'Pike', *Lupercal* (Faber, 1960). Reproduced by permission of the Estate of Ted Hughes and of Faber and Faber Ltd. Extract from 'Pike' from *COLLECTED POEMS* by Ted Hughes. Copyright © 2003 by The Estate of Ted Hughes. Reprinted by permission of Farrar, Straus and Giroux. All Rights Reserved.

E.A. Markham: Extract from 'Epilogue', *Looking Out, Looking In: New and Selected Poems* (Anvil Press Poetry, 2009). Reproduced by kind permission of Carcanet Press, Manchester, UK.

Paul Mills: Extract from 'Flight Back', *Dinosaur Point* (Smith/Doorstop, 2000). Reprinted by kind permission of Smith/Doorstop Books. www.poetrybusiness.co.uk.

Daljit Nagra: Extract from 'Ode to England', *British Museum* (Faber, 2017). Reproduced by permission of the author and of Faber and Faber Ltd.

Grace Nichols: Extract from 'Outward from Hull', *Picasso, I Want My Face Back* (Bloodaxe, 2014). Reproduced with permission of Bloodaxe Books. www.bloodaxe.com.

Alice Oswald: Extract from *Dart* (Faber, 2002). Reproduced by permission of the author and of Faber and Faber Ltd. Extract from *Dart* by Alice Oswald (© Wendy Cope, 2002) is printed by permission of United Agents (www.unitedagents.co.uk) on behalf of Alice Oswald.